Edmond Zi-Kang Chua

'God-ness', 'God-ity', and God

A Historical Study and Synthesis of the
Christian Doctrine of the Divine Being

UNIVERSITY PRESS
OF THE SOUTH

2022

Copyright © 2022 by Chua Zi Kang

All rights reserved. No part of this publication may be reproduced, stored in a retrieval system, or transmitted, in any form or by any means, electronic, mechanical, photocopying, recording or otherwise, without the prior written permission of the Publisher.

Published in the United States by:
The University Press of the South
E-mail: unprsouth@aol.com; universitypresssouth@gmail.com
Visit our award-winning web pages: www.unprsouth.com
www.punouveaumonde.com

Printed in France by Monbeaulivre.fr

Edmond Zi-Kang Chua
'God-ness', 'God-ity', and God. A Historical Study and Synthesis of the Christian Doctrine of the Divine Being
Second edition in English
xiv + 128 pages. Religious Studies Series, 41
Front Cover Art: Carving, Salisbury Cathedral (England). Photo by Katharine Hunt. Reproduced with permission.

1. Christianity 2. Christian Doctrine 3. Trinity Dogma 4. God-ness 5. God-ity 6. Colin Ewart Gunton 7. Thomas Allan Smail 8. John Zizioulas 9. Basil of Caesarea 10. Gregory of Nazianzus

ISBN: 978-1-937030-62-9 (First edition: USA, 2015)
ISBN: 978-1-952799-40-2 (Second edition: Europe, 2022)

To the memory of David Eng Mong Chua (October 8, 1947–September 27, 2015),

a man loving with the Spirit of my Lord Jesus,
the only begotten Son of God,
now and forevermore with his blessed Father

Abstract

A groundbreaking solution to the ageless three-one problematic of the logical coherence of the Christian doctrine of the Trinity, *'God-ness', 'God-ity', and God: A Historical Study and Synthesis of the Christian Doctrine of the Divine Being* tracks down and formulates two major conceptions of the idea of 'God' in patristic and modern Christian theology, 'God' variously understood in terms of nature and relationship, and unifies them in a dazzlingly novel, tradition-based notion of a "perichoretic constitution".

According to this illuminating formulation, the divine Trinity is re-imagined as a community of three ontologically dependent entities, a proto-Father, proto-Son, and proto-Holy Spirit. Each of these proto-persons possesses a unique principle of wisdom, will, and agency of action, giving and receiving access to each other's unique principles to allow each single proto-person to be fully constituted as divine person embedded in an ontological framework arising from a communion of being.

In this manner, each divine person may be understood to be fully God, and the only God, because formed in this way from the exhaustive divinity of the ontology-forming fellowship of the three, "Though there are three divine persons, there is only one God;" and this only God is not simply one but generated by the community of three jointly-full divine persons, "Though there is only one God, there are three divine persons."

Contents

Abstract iv
In Clarification vii
In Acknowledgement viii
Preface ix
    Object x
    Method xi
    A Note on Style xi
Abbreviations xii
Introduction 1
    Major Interpretations of the Concept of the Being of God 2
    Theologians Behind Theologies of Divine Being 4
Part 1: Theologians of 'God-ness' 5
    Chapter 1: Basil of Caesarea, A 6
        Liber de Spiritu Sancto 6
        Epistula 38 (Attribution of Convenience) 12
    Chapter 2: Basil of Caesarea, B 18
        Epistula 214 18
        Epistula 236 27
    Chapter 3: Gregory of Nazianzus 30
        Oratio 29 30
        Oratio 31 32
        Oratio 39 38
        Oratio 40 40
    Chapter 4: Gregory of Nyssa 41
        De Sancta Trinitate 41
        Ad Ablabium 46
        Ad Graecos 54

Chapter 5: Augustine of Hippo and Other Theologians 59
    De Trinitate 59
    Other Theologians 61

Part 2: Theologians of 'God-ity' 65
    Chapter 6: John D. Zizioulas, Colin E. Gunton, and Thomas A. Smail 70
        John D. Zizioulas 70
        Colin E. Gunton 73
        Thomas A. Smail 76

Part 3: A Proposal 79
    Chapter 7: Finding a Place for the One in the Three: The Procrustean Bed of Trinitarian Theology 80
        A Problem Unresolved 81
        A Possible Solution: *Perichoretic Constitution* 83
            Biblical Basis 93
            Doctrinal Basis 95
        An Important Objection Refuted 99
    Chapter 8: Implications: Scriptural, Doctrinal, Ethical, Missional, and Practical 103
        Scriptural Implications 103
        Doctrinal Implications 105
        Ethical Implications 108
        Missional Implications 109
        Practical Implications 110

Conclusion 112
Bibliography 113

In Clarification

I wish to use this section to issue a clarification pursuant to a statement made in a review of the present work which appeared in *Reviews in Religion and Theology*, Vol. 23, Issue 3, July 2016, pp. 276-79.

First of all, I would like to express my deep gratitude to the reviewer, Adetunbi Richard Ogunleye (PhD, Ambrose Alli University), affiliated at the time of the review with the Adekunle Ajasin University in Nigeria, for a summary of the content of my book. I would like, however, to advert to the final sentence of the penultimate paragraph of the review in which the reviewer writes, "However, the author could not achieve his goal as various objections and implications were raised."

This comment appears to be a reference to the section in the seventh chapter entitled, "An Important Objection Considered", as well as the focus of the discussion of the eighth, which has in view the implications of the doctrine developed in my book.

I should like to intimate, respectfully, that in the section to which I have adverted, "An Important Objection Considered", I have done more than simply consider a vital objection; indeed, I mounted an effective rebuttal of the specific objection in question. Furthermore, I believe that my work has succeeded rather than failed at formulating a doctrine of the Trinity which logically and coherently incorporates both the monotheistic idea of God as a single personal being and a Trinitarian one involving an acknowledgment of the full divinity of the Father, Son, and Holy Spirit as being in their own right.

For avoidance of all doubt, therefore, I have elected to rename the section in question, "An Important Objection Refuted". Finally, the eighth chapter addresses itself to implications of the doctrine I have developed and not those of the opposing doctrine.

In Acknowledgement

The result of a drawn-out and personal search for a viable solution to the ostensible logical paradox of the Christian doctrine of the Trinity, this very book might not have come into existence without the positive feedback given by an editor of the *Journal of Theological Studies* published by Oxford University Press. I had submitted a shorter manuscript for consideration of publication in the *JTS,* and Graham Gould (PhD, Cantab) responded with an in-depth review of my work on 23 July 2015.

In his critique, Dr. Gould commented on the comprehensive scope of the discussion and the "radical" originality of the coinage of the idea of "proto-divine persons" and a theory concerning how in a purely logical sequence they obtain each other's unique principles, observing that I employ these conceptions to bring together a substance and relational understanding of the divine being, remarking that in view of these aspects, the shorter manuscript at the time was, in his informed and professional estimation, "a very good and stimulating piece of work."

The *JTS* editor proceeded to explain at length why he deemed the manuscript submission unsuitable as a prospective journal article, and ultimately urged the reworking of the manuscript through expansion and amendments on areas specifically highlighted in the form of a book.

I have taken assiduous care in attending to the issues broached by Dr. Gould by way of dilating on the original material, which preserves the original final thesis, in such a way as to constitute a full-length monograph.

Preface

There are a variety of conceptions of the single personal being of God[1] in light of triple personhood. By the Cappadocian Fathers and Augustine of Hippo throughout their writings on the Trinity, God is posited as nature.[2] The being of God is equated in the thought of Tertullian, Origen, and Eusebius of Caesarea with the person of the Father.[3] Karl Barth conceives of God as a particular state of the divine persons.[4] Pseudo-Cyril of Alexandria avers that God comprises the identity common to the divine persons.[5] In the writings of John Zizioulas, Colin Gunton, and Thomas Smail, one is confronted with the idea of the divine being as relational dynamic.[6]

Up until now, Christian theologians are presented in the doctrine of the Trinity with the unique twofold challenge of articulating tenets of a belief which, in the eyes of many, has not seen satisfactory internal synthesis, judging from references to a lack of understanding surrounding the doctrine[7] and attempts right up to the present time to comprehend afresh what it means to refer to God as single or formulate a scripturally

---

[1] R. A. te Velde, 'The Divine Person(s): Trinity, Person, and Analogous Naming', in *The Oxford Handbook of the Trinity*, ed. G. Emery and M. Levering (Oxford: Oxford University Press, 2011), p. 359.

[2] See, for instance, Basil of Caesarea, *Spir.* 18.44; Gregory of Nazianzus, *Or.* 29.2; Gregory of Nyssa, *Abl.*; and Augustine of Hippo, *Trin.* 7.9.

[3] According to G. L. Prestige, *God in Patristic Thought* (Eugene, OR: Wipf & Stock, 2008), pp. 98–99, 132–33, 142–45.

[4] According to E. Jüngel, *God's Being Is In Becoming: The Trinitarian Being of God in the Theology of Karl Barth. A Paraphrase*, trans. J. Webster (Grand Rapids, MI: William B. Eerdmans, 2001), pp. 42–45.

[5] Prestige, *God in Patristic Thought*, pp. 284, 295–301.

[6] See, for instance, J. D. Zizioulas, *Being as Communion: Studies in Personhood and the Church*, CGT 4 (Crestwood, NY: St. Vladimir's Seminary Press, 1985), p. 17; C. E. Gunton, *The Promise of Trinitarian Theology*, 2nd ed. (London: T&T Clark, 1997), pp. 8–11; T. A. Smail, *Like Father, Like Son: The Trinity Imaged in Our Humanity* (Milton Keynes, UK: Paternoster, 2005), pp. 137–41, 147–50.

[7] A case in point is T. George, introduction to *God the Holy Trinity: Reflections on Christian Faith and Practice*, ed. T. George (Grand Rapids, MI: Baker Academic, 2006), p. 9. Of note also is the skepticism of Maurice Wiles pertaining to the possibility of reconciling arguments mounted in the third and fourth centuries in support of differentiation and oneness in the Godhead respectively. M. Wiles, *The Making of Christian Doctrine* (Cambridge: Cambridge University Press, 1967), p. 124 (cited in S. Coakley, 'Why Three? Some Further Reflections on the Origins of the Doctrine of the Trinity', in *The Making and Remaking of Christian Doctrine: Essays in Honour of Maurice Wiles*, ed. S. Coakley and D. A. Pailin [Oxford: Clarendon Press, 1993], pp. 29–30).

accurate analogy of the triune nature of God that bears explanatory value,[8] and expounding it.

Major theologians from the fourth century on have taken seriously implicit New Testament affirmations regarding the full deity of the Father, the Son, and the Holy Spirit. From that standpoint, they have sought to do justice to the truth claim, also present in Scripture, to the effect that the deity is also one. Their definitions of what can be called the divine being have been a significant contribution to theological discourse concerning the nature of God as they hold the promise of reconciling in a coherent whole the ideas of God as three and yet as one.

Concurrently, there is also a sense of optimism that the Trinity can finally be coherently formulated as expressed by Brian Edgar at the beginning of his biblical exposition of the Trinity in speaking about the doctrine as being devoid of any real obscurity.[9] Some are sounding a clarion call to take up the immanent Trinity as a subject for exploration as one of eight tasks that form the core of thinking about the Trinity in the present time.[10]

Object

This study has been undertaken with a view to commending the Christian doctrine of the Trinity in its metaphysical and ontological dimension as logically acceptable and intelligible without sacrificing scriptural faithfulness. A critical assumption is that this goal has not to date been achieved.

To be sure, as the previous section has briefly demonstrated, various conceptions of the being of God have been propounded, all of which pass the test of logical coherence. Whether, however, these same proposals will also be found to be completely consistent with the biblical revelation of the divine being is a different question altogether. The claim that undergirds this conspectus is that there is probably no existing exposition that can adequately account for both the one and three in God. Admittedly, this is an

---

[8] J. Macnamara, M. La Palme Reyes, and G. E. Reyes, 'Logic and the Trinity', *Faith and Philosophy* 11 (1994), p. 7 (cited in J. S. Feinberg, *No One Like Him: The Doctrine of God*, Foundations of Evangelical Theology [Wheaton, IL: Crossway Books, 2001], pp. 496–98).

[9] B. Edgar, *The Message of the Trinity: Life in God*, The Bible Speaks Today (Leicester, UK: Inter-Varsity, 2004), p. 20.

[10] G. Emery and M. Levering, "Prospects for Trinitarian Theology," in *The Oxford Handbook of the Trinity*, ed. G. Emery and M. Levering (Oxford: Oxford University Press, 2011), pp. 604–5.

argument not from a positive demonstration that no such works exist, but an inference, grounded in the observation, already noted above, that scholars continue to grapple with the doctrine on a logical and conceptual level.

Nonetheless, lack of clear and undeniable evidence that the logical question of the immanent Trinity has been satisfactorily resolved should not inhibit academic exploration of a better way of understanding the doctrine, even if such a venture has to be justified by a mere assumption.

Method

To achieve the object of this study, an attempt will be made to synthesize existing conceptions in the hope of uncovering a way to outline a scheme which neglects neither the one nor three in the divine being. Such an approach entails certain corollaries.

Solely those proposals which are useful for the formulation of a logically coherent and scripturally faithful scheme will be considered to any depth. Furthermore, the search for helpful proposals will end as soon as a sufficient number of them has been identified. Although the conceptual accuracy of these ideas will be shown via a survey and analysis of texts from its proponents, this validation will not interact exhaustively or even comprehensively with scholarship touching on those conceptions.

This, again, is due to the focused nature and clear object of the study, which is to develop a proposal concerning the divine being by building on existing schemes. In addition, the choice of theologians for study will not be grounded in any particular rationale, though the Cappadocian Fathers have been selected for their historical role in the formulation of the Trinitarian doctrine.[11]

A Note on Style

References to 'the writer' are usually to the author of this study.

---

[11] R. P. C. Hanson, *The Search for the Christian Doctrine of God: The Arian Controversy, 318—381* (Edinburgh: T. & T. Clark, 1988), p. 676 (cited in M. L. Chiavone, *The One God: A Critically Developed Evangelical Doctrine of Trinitarian Unity* [Eugene, OR: Pickwick, 2009], p. 17).

Abbreviations

AAR	American Academy of Religion
AB	Anchor Bible
Abl.	*Ad Ablabium*
ACD	Ancient Christian Doctrine
Apol.	*Liber Apologeticus*
C. Ar.	*Orationes contra Arianos*
Catech.	*Oratio catechetica*
Comm. not.	*Adversus Graecos ex communibus notionibus*
Dial.	*Dialectica*
Ep.	*Epistulae*
Eun.	*Contra Eunomium*
Exp. fid.	*Expositio fidei*
FC	Fathers of the Church
GNO	Gregorii Nysseni opera
GOTR	*Greek Orthodox Theological Review*
HTR	*Harvard Theological Review*

JTS	*The Journal of Theological Studies*
LCL	Loeb Classical Library
Mon.	*Monologium*
NPNF	Nicene and Post-Nicene Fathers
NZSTh	*Neue Zeitschrift Für Systematische Theologie Und Religionsphilosophie*
OCC	Open Court Classics
OECS	Oxford Early Christian Studies
OECT	Oxford Early Christian Texts
OSHT	Oxford Studies in Historical Theology
Or.	*Orationes*
PG	Patrologia Graeca
PGL	*A Patristic Greek Lexicon*
PPS	Popular Patristics Series
Sanct. Trin.	*De Sancta Trinitate*
SJT	*Scottish Journal of Theology*
Spir.	*Liber de Spiritu Sancto*
ST	*Summa Theologiae*

Trin.	*De Trinitate*
TS	*Theological Studies*
Utr. Pat.	*Utrum Pater et Filius et Spiritus Sanctus De Divinitate substantialiter praedicentur*
VC	*Vigiliae Christianae*
VCSup	Vigiliae Christianae Supplement Series
WSA	The Works of St. Augustine: A Translation for the 21st Century
ZAC	*Zeitschrift für Antikes Christentum*

Introduction

Enshrined in the fourth century Niceno-Constantinopolitan Creed[1] subscribed to by Christians from across the three traditions, to wit, Roman Catholicism, Eastern Orthodoxy and Protestantism, the belief that the sole deity, whom Jews and then Christians worshipped, exists in three forms, namely the Father, Son, and Holy Spirit,[2] has the status of settled doctrine. A common and widely accepted formulation[3] uses the terminology of being and personhood to distinguish between that which is single and unified in the godhead and that which is triple and differentiated in the same.

Utilizing the concepts of being and personhood, the doctrine of the Trinity can be summed up by a reference to God in the Christian understanding as being the only God, who has existed eternally in three persons, each of whom possesses the fullness of divine being in distinctive relations to the others, without constituting three autonomous deities or gods since there is a mutual interpenetration of the three persons in which each is an integral part of the others, and the others an integral part of each in such a manner that

---

[1] See, for instance, the translation of the Greek text printed by G. L. Dossetti in *Il Simbolo di Nicea e di Constantinopoli*, pp. 244ff by R. P. C. Hanson in *The Search for the Christian Doctrine of God: The Arian Controversy, 318—381* (Grand Rapids, MI: Baker Academic, 2005), pp. 815–16.

[2] While the Creed of Constantinople does not explicitly state that the Holy Spirit is consubstantial with the Father and the Son, the idea is implicitly present. See J. Behr, *The Nicene Faith*, vol. 2 of *The Formation of Christian Theology* (Crestwood, NY: St. Vladimir's Seminary Press, 2004), 2:378–79.

[3] Some attempts to make a distinction between God in His oneness and threeness try to eschew the language of personhood altogether, such as that of Rahner. See K. Rahner, *The Trinity*, trans. J. Donceel (New York: Crossroad, 1997), p. 110 (cited in R. Letham, *The Holy Trinity: In Scripture, History, Theology, and Worship* [Phillipsburg, NJ: P&R, 2004], p. 295) and P. C. Phan, 'Developments of the doctrine of the Trinity', in *The Cambridge Companion to The Trinity*, ed. P. C. Phan (Cambridge: Cambridge University Press, 2011), p. 6. Colin Gunton notes Barth's distinctive approach in *Becoming and Being: The Doctrine of God in Charles Hartshorne and Karl Barth*, 2nd ed. (London: SCM, 2001), p. 141.

it is appropriate and necessary to conceive of the three persons not individually but as a single being.

Beyond this general framework, there is more to be said in regard to the meaning of the concept of the being or substance of God in light of his triple personhood. This is one of the key ways in which the doctrine has developed through the history of Christianity, as this study will demonstrate.

While headway has decidedly been made in Christian understanding of the triune nature of God, particularly in furnishing theologians with adequate conceptual tools with which to attain greater dogmatic clarity, in one estimation the enterprise still anticipates a reconciliation of the ideas of divine being with personhood. It will be shown that this can be achieved by a coming to terms with the ontological interdependence of the persons in the godhead.

The outline of this study is as follows: First, two major interpretations[4] of the meaning of the concept of the being of God[5] will be identified and introduced. In separate sections, it will be established that these views were indeed held by prominent theologians. Second, that those perspectives provide the conditions for the development of a third which complements them will be demonstrated. Finally, that third view will be propounded.

Major Interpretations of the Concept of the Being of God

In the course of the history of Trinitarian doctrine, numerous ways of understanding the being of God have been suggested. One sees being as referring to individual makeup

---

[4] These interpretations are selected on the basis of their ability to form a trajectory along which a hopefully fuller conception of the divine being may be developed.

[5] This is primarily a study of the dominant ways in which theologians have sought to reconcile what is three and what is one in the Trinity via a definition of divine oneness which is able to accommodate a preexisting conception of divine three-ness. Due to the conceptual nature of the study, minimal reference will be made to Greek and Latin terminology used to denote what is three and what is one in God; instead, ideas employed to signify the one and three in the Trinity will be identified, and given the general terms, in the case of the one, 'divine being', 'being of God', 'divine essence', 'divine substance', 'divine oneness', all used interchangeably in reference to that which God is; and, in the case of the three, 'divine person', 'divine entity', used interchangeably in reference to that which the Father, Son or Holy Spirit is.

and orientation. The Cappadocian Fathers and Augustine of Hippo are among proponents of this view, who interpret being in terms of nature, qualities[6], and desire.

In this understanding, the oneness of God is not a numerical oneness as opposed to the numerical reference to God as three persons. It is a qualitative oneness, and yet one which unites the numerically three persons both substantially and in the dimension of purpose. The three divine persons are exactly the same in regard to their omnipotence, omniscience, omnipresence, eternity, righteousness, and love. Moreover they are of exactly the same mind and have the same will, purpose, and action. Accordingly, to speak of the oneness of the being of God amounts to speaking of a sameness of the substance, will, and action of the three divine persons, of 'God-ness'.[7]

A second perspective posits the being of God as relational dynamic. Advocates of this point of view, including J. D. Zizioulas, C. E. Gunton, and T. A. Smail, conceptualize the being of God not in terms of individual makeup and orientation, but of the relationships the divine persons share. This makes the interpersonal dynamic essential to the being of God, thus allowing one to speak of oneness in the manner of participation without sacrificing ontology.

The divine being, then, is not so much to be conceived as the common nature of individual entities, but a complex of interaction, rooted in the fact and governing principle that the promise or potential of each divine person is ineluctably and eternally tied to the presence and wellbeing of the others. On this view, the relationship between the being of God and the divine persons is somewhat analogous to that between the concept of humanity and human persons. Consequently, God is to be understood as the perfect community, mutuality, and solidarity that already and unceasingly exists between the Father, Son, and Holy Spirit. In this outlook, to speak of the oneness of God is to speak of the oneness of a principle of wellbeing, shared life, and community, of 'God-ity'.

There are obviously other theologies of divine being, such as those which equate the being of God with the person of the Father, posit the divine being as a particular state of the divine persons, or resolve the question of the unity of the divine essence by recourse to a redefinition of the concept of the divine being as the identity common to the divine persons. These being plainly theologically or ontologically reductionist, and, more importantly, not fundamentally necessary for the attainment of the object of the

---

[6] Of a particular substance. This is how the idea of 'quality' in regard to the substantive view of the being of God is used throughout this study.

[7] This notion also surfaces in K. DeYoung, *The Good News We Almost Forgot: Rediscovering the Gospel in a 16th Catechism* (Chicago: Moody, 2010), p. 50.

study,[8] they shall be dealt with only in passing, sometimes as part of the main argument, sometimes as peripheral to the central thesis.

Theologians Behind Theologies of Divine Being

The first two sections will attempt to show that the perspectives of divine being as individual makeup and orientation, and of being as relational dynamic were actually held by theologians.

---

[8] On which, see pertinent section in the preface.

Part 1

Theologians of 'God-ness'

Leaders from the Western and Eastern parts of the fourth century church alike were agreed that the being of God points to the substance that constitutes the divine persons and is possessed by them, and to their identical will, purpose, and action.

This study will focus on the theologies of Basil of Caesarea, Gregory of Nazianzus, Gregory of Nyssa, and Augustine of Hippo.

Chapter 1

Basil of Caesarea, A

Liber de Spiritu Sancto

A clear grasp of the single and triple dimensions of the Trinity can be found in the thought of Basil of Caesarea,[1] who is persuaded that unlike the gods in polytheistic systems, the Father, the Son, and the Holy Spirit cannot be enumerated as though they were separate and individual entities in such a way as to suggest that there are three divine beings or Gods.

The reason Basil furnishes in the eighteenth chapter of his *Liber de Spiritu Sancto*[2] for cautioning against enumerating the divine persons in the way that polytheists count their gods is that whenever the majesty of the divine persons is contemplated and revered ultimately it is one and the same being that is being contemplated and revered, because the divine persons share in the same being.

If, as he seems to be implying in the following paragraph,[3] it is the singleness of the divine being that causes all worship to be directed not in three ways but in one way, at the divine being itself, is Basil then suggesting that worship is directed at what is impersonal rather than what is personal? Zizioulas resolves this conundrum by underlining

---

[1] P. Kariatlis, 'St Basil's Contribution to the Trinitarian Doctrine: A Synthesis of Greek *Paideia* and the Scriptural Worldview', *Phronema* 25 (2010), p. 58. *ATLA Religion Database with ATLASerials*, EBSCO*host* (accessed February 27, 2015).

[2] Basil of Caesarea, *Spir.* 18.44. The translation by Stephen Hildebrand in the Popular Patristics Series was used.

[3] Basil of Caesarea, *Spir.* 18.45.

what he sees as a distinctive Eastern church emphasis on the person of the Father as the very being of God through drawing out the implications of the statement, which Basil makes[4] and which is also found in the opening line of the Creed of Constantinople, to the effect that the Father is the one God.[5]

This, coupled with the illustration from the king and the king's image which Basil employs,[6] illuminates the point he is attempting to make: worship directed towards either the Son or the Holy Spirit is also by extension directed towards the Father, whose being is identical to that of the Son and the Holy Spirit,[7] and who is the cause or origin, though not ontologically but relationally[8]—and not in the sense in which Zizioulas uses it, namely, as the factor which causes change, and not according to his framework which conflates the divine nature and hierarchy, thus making the hierarchy ontological and defining it as a flow of the divine nature from the Father to the Son and Spirit—of the Son and the Holy Spirit.

The concepts of being unbegotten or begetting, *spirating*, being a cause, source, or origin; only begotten; and proceeding or being *spirated*, the first of which is classified under the category of causing or generating, and the latter two of which fall under the category of being caused or generated, are to be taken[9] as denotative[10] of the central roles of

---

[4] Such as in Basil of Caesarea, *Spir.* 18.44.

[5] Zizioulas, *Being as Communion*, pp. 40–41.

[6] Basil of Caesarea, *Spir.* 18.45 (Hildebrand, PPS).

[7] Accordingly, Basil writes in *Spir.* 18.44 that the church preaches the divine persons in exactly the same manner, as having one nature (ʼμοναχ-ῶς', *LSJ* 2:1143). Basil of Caesarea, *Spir.* 18 (PG 32:44a).

[8] R. Letham, *The Holy Trinity: In Scripture, History, Theology, and Worship* (Phillipsburg, NJ: P&R, 2004), pp. 154–55, 159, 162, 165.

[9] These terms are most probably synonymous. E. P. Meijering identifies the generation and causation of the Son by the Father, in *God Being History: Studies in Patristic Philosophy* (Amsterdam: North-Holland, 1975), p. 109, n. 34. Lucian Turcescu in 'Person', in *The Brill Dictionary of Gregory of Nyssa*, ed. L. F. Mateo-Seco and G. Maspero, trans. S. Cherney, Supplements to VCSup 99 (Boston: Brill, 2010), p. 593, equates the notions of origin and causation in the divine being with that of generation, begetting and *spiration*. Giulio Maspero in 'Trinity' in *The Brill Dictionary of Gregory of Nyssa*, ed. L. F. Mateo-Seco and G. Maspero, trans. S. Cherney, VCSup 99 (Boston: Brill, 2010), p. 756, highlights from Gregory of Nyssa, *Abl.* GNO 3.1:56.11–22 that Gregory himself identifies causation, in the context of the immanent Trinity, with generation.

[10] To designate the divine persons using verbs of relationship is apt for those whose very names signify relation in their most complete form: the Father is actually shorthand for 'the Father of the Son' (see 1 Pet. 1:3); the Son for 'the Son of the Father' (see 1 John 4:15); and the Holy Spirit for 'the Spirit of the Father' (see Eph. 3:14–16), or 'the Spirit of the Son' (see Gal. 4:6). Note the related discussion in J. Moltmann, *The Trinity and the Kingdom: The Doctrine of God,*

Father, Son and Holy Spirit respectively to which the divine persons have always committed.[11] These terms function as metaphors for identity of essence between the producer and the produced—a signification that is to the fore in Athanasius' theology,[12] at least in the case of relational terms applied between the Father and the Son—for the distinctive mutually complementary relationships into which each enters, and for the distinction between the Son, who is begotten, and the Spirit, who is *spirated*, and the created order, the members of which are, of course, created.[13]

As a case in point, the concept of begetting signifies a physical process by which a male parent produces an offspring of the same nature by means of sexual intercourse with another, and consequently enters into a paternal relationship with that offspring, who, in turn, enters into a filial relationship with the male parent. With the divine persons, non-physical and uncreated as they are, there is no real process of generation, only the designation by the concept, say, of begetting of the identity of the natures of the Father and Son, and of the paternal relationship into which the former has eternally entered with the latter, and of the filial relationship into which the latter has eternally entered with the former.

In contradiction to the foregoing, Meesters is fairly certain that the Cappadocian Fathers espoused no such doctrine as an internal hierarchy within the Trinity. He highlights Basil's concept of the difference between the Father and the Son as non-temporal and non-ontological but purely conceptual. Although he allows for a flow of authority in regard to divine acts, presumably, upon creation, there is no notion of distinctive self-identities in which one conceives of oneself as being lower or higher in rank than another.[14]

---

trans. M. Kohl (Minneapolis, MN: Fortress Press, 1993), pp. 162–63, 183. Also see Turcescu, 'Person', p. 593.

[11] For a statement of what it means to conceive of Father, Son and Holy Spirit as roles and why it is necessary to do so, see the section discussing the theology of Gregory Nyssen.

[12] Athanasius of Alexandria, *C. Ar.* 2.34 (Newman and Robertson, *NPNF*² 4:366) and idem., *C. Ar.* 3.4 (Newman and Robertson, *NPNF*² 4:395).

[13] R. Letham, 'Eternal Generation in the Church Fathers', in *One God in Three Persons: Unity of Essence, Distinction of Persons, Implications for Life*, ed. B. A. Ware and J. Starke (Wheaton, IL: Crossway, 2015), pp. 119–21.

[14] A. C. Meesters, 'The Cappadocians and Their Trinitarian Conceptions of God', *NZSTh* 54, no. 4 (2012), p. 411. *ATLA Religion Database with ATLASerials*, EBSCO*host* (accessed August 1, 2015).

To assert this, however, is to beg the question of what a conceptual precedence[15] of the Father relative to the Son and the Holy Spirit, concerning the immanent Trinity, consists in if it is not relational or functional. Is the distinction between the persons merely formal, without any meaningful content whatsoever? Are the names of the Father, Son, and Holy Spirit bereft of all substance, so that the use of any other series of three names would equally have sufficed, as long as they denote by their difference the fact that there are three rather than two entities or just one? Or do they indicate differing statuses, even within the Godhead?

In the opinion of David Brown, there is a definite differentiation of status between the Father and the Son, who are not rather called associates.[16] Wayne Grudem takes the same view.[17] There appears to be a tacit assumption on the part of Meesters that ontological equality among the divine persons is antithetical to distinction in rank.[18] Therefore he takes great pains to dissociate the theology of the Cappadocians from certain supposedly infelicitous language employed both in the original Nicene Creed and by Gregory of Nazianzus in his earlier days.[19] At any rate, there is no contradiction between qualitative ontological identity and differential statuses.

To insist on their fundamental incompatibility is to reveal another undergirding presupposition: that difference in rank necessarily reflects ontological difference. Yet position does not denote ontological distinction; this is the case even in the human world. Great and authoritarian as he is, the father remains a human being, no different in that respect from his son, over whom he has authority. It is granted that with human fatherhood there is an element of biological determination that does not hold with divine paternity. The first person of the Trinity is not Father by nature, or the second, Son in virtue of a process of genetic reproduction. The Father is Father by choice, albeit an eternal and unchanging decision, to exist in this manner in regard to the Son, who is also Son by eternal self-determination. If relational distinctions within the Godhead are a matter not of nature but of decision, these distinctions may coexist with ontological equality.

---

[15] Ibid., p. 396.

[16] D. Brown, *The Divine Trinity* (La Salle, IL: Open Court, 1985), p. 283.

[17] W. Grudem, *Evangelical Feminism and Biblical Truth* (Sisters, OR: Multnomah, 2004), p. 413 (cited in T. H. McCall, *Which Trinity? Whose Monotheism? Philosophical and Systematic Theologians on the Metaphysics of Trinitarian Theology* [Grand Rapids, MI: William B. Eerdmans, 2010], p. 183).

[18] Brown, *Divine Trinity*, pp. 396–413.

[19] Ibid., pp. 407–408.

At this point, an explanation of the insistence on an unreservedly 'relational- denotative' view of the terms used to indicate relations of origin between the divine persons is in order. Might it not be propounded that there is something more to, say, the 'begetting' of the Son by the Father than the function and role it specifies? Can it not have any reference to an eternal 'act' of some sort, like one in which the Father communicates his substance to the Son and the Holy Spirit? This option is excluded on the basis that in eternity no act is possible, since an act by definition involves the idea of time, and of a beginning of the action. For this reason, it is better to speak of 'states' than 'acts' in regard to eternity.

Furthermore, an ontological view of the causation of divine persons is fundamentally incompatible with the claim of their identity of substance, a point Mullins has lucidly demonstrated, albeit seemly in support of the jettisoning of the doctrine of eternal generation of the Son.[20] Hence, the terms are better seen as denotative of relationship and function than ontological distinction.[21]

Zizioulas' dichotomization of divine being against divine substance is to be understood in light of the fact that he is making a protest not against the concept of substance *per se* but the concept of substance abstracted or divorced from personhood. As he elucidates the stand of the Greek fathers, he does not dispense with the concept of substance.[22]

In the final analysis, worship can only be offered to that which is personal, in other words, to the divine persons, and not to the underlying impersonal substance or nature within the persons. Indeed, the substance can only be considered by looking at the persons, since the substance or nature resides only in the person and not 'nakedly', as Zizioulas observes.[23]

---

[20] R. T. Mullins, 'An Analytic Response to Stephen R. Holmes, with a Special Treatment of his Doctrine of Divine Simplicity', in *The Holy Trinity Revisited: Essays in Response to Stephen R. Holmes*, ed. T. A. Noble and J. S. Sexton, Christian Doctrines in Historical Perspective (Milton Keynes, England: Paternoster, 2015), pp. 92–94.

[21] Be that as it may, some writers continue to employ the concept of act or at least the nomenclature, like J. A. McGuckin in "Perceiving Light from Light in Light' (*Oration* 31.3): The Trinitarian Theology of Saint Gregory the Theologian', in *GOTR* 39, no. 1 (1994), p. 27. *ATLA Religion Database with ATLASerials*, EBSCO*host* (accessed August 13, 2015).

[22] Zizioulas, *Being as Communion*, pp. 41–42, n. 37. The same view is held in regard to the divine being by the Greek father Athanasius, highlights Prestige in *God in Patristic Thought* (Eugene, OR: Wipf & Stock, 2008), p. 195.

[23] Zizioulas, *Being as Communion*, p. 41.

Nonetheless, Basil is not thereby defining the being of God in terms of the personhood of the Father, seeing that he speaks of divine nature and the complete resemblance between the Father and the Son.[24] In his understanding, the divine being is a part of the personal reality of the divine persons which deserves adoration; it is not identical to personhood, as Zizioulas claims. When he speaks of the worship of God, he is referring to the adoration of the three persons as equally divine.

In regard to the assertion in *Spir.* 18.44 to the effect that there is one God and Father, one only begotten, and one Holy Spirit, the term of particular importance, εἷς, and ἕν,[25] is more clearly understood as a group identity marker of the divine and spiritual,[26] expressing both the complete equivalence of group members, as well as their complete uniqueness that sets them apart from any other entity. Rendering the statement with a view to bringing out such a sense would result in the following explanatory addition to the statement: 'There is a group of three divine entities, a Trinity: one God and Father and one only begotten and one Holy Spirit, each having a substance that is common and unique to them.'

Although the idea of the Father as the one 'God' remains, it is now qualified by the indication that this 'God' belongs in a group along with two equally divine and unique others. In this way, the word 'God' is relativized, and becomes a name akin to 'Father', 'Only-begotten', 'Holy Spirit',[27] obviating, in a more fundamental way, the problem John Behr perceives of a weakening by a doctrine of the Father as the one God of the divinity of the other two persons.[28] For this reason, contrary to the claim of the same that Basil

---

[24] Basil of Caesarea, *Spir.* 18.45. This is also the view of Prestige, shown in his comment on the passage in *God in Patristic Thought*, p. 230. Here, then, can be observed a departure, noted by Prestige, from an earlier notion of the divine monarchy as revolving around the equation of the divine being with the person of the Father. Ibid., pp. 98–99, 132–33, 233, 254, 258.

[25] Basil of Caesarea, *Spir.* 18 (PG 32:44a).

[26] 'εἷς', *PGL* 470.

[27] Ware shows how Paul himself, in his benediction in 2 Cor. 13:14, uses the name of God to indicate the person of the Father as an alternate name, though he reaches the conclusion that the other sense in which the apostle uses the name is that of the Trinity rather than the nature of the Trinity. B. A. Ware, *Father, Son, and Holy Spirit: Relationships, Roles and Relevance* (Wheaton, IL: Crossway Books, 2005), pp. 40, 159. Centuries earlier, Augustine of Hippo made the same observation. Augustine of Hippo, *Trin.* 1.12 (Hill, WSA; cited in L. Gioia, *The Theological Epistemology of Augustine's De Trinitate*, Oxford Theological Monographs [Oxford: Oxford University Press, 2008], p. 163).

[28] Behr, *Nicene Faith*, 2:307.

holds to such a view of the divine being,[29] the being of God may be defined using the category of nature or substance.

The being of God, therefore, is that which is common to and distinctive of the divine persons. To define divine being in terms of nature or makeup, orientation, and action is to be consistent with the meaning and connotation of the concepts of divine nature and complete resemblance between divine persons, ideas employed by Basil.[30]

Epistula 38 (Attribution of Convenience)

As the theologian who bequeathed to the church her cherished and familiar way of expressing the triune nature of God, μία οὐσία, τρεῖς ὑποστάσεις,[31] Basil infused the words οὐσία and ὑπόστασις, which along with ὕπαρξις (in one of its senses), were the three words in fourth-century Greek for an existent object,[32] with new meaning; in the first case, the new sense had to do with a oneness of nature; and in the second, a distinctive form.[33]

His prowess as an incisive theological thinker is on dazzling display in one of his epistolary correspondences with his brother Gregory of Nyssa,[34] in which he tries to

---

[29] Ibid.

[30] Basil of Caesarea, *Spir.* 18.45 (Hildebrand, PPS).

[31] R. J. Deferrari, introduction to *Basil: The Letters 1—58*, by Basil of Caesarea, LCL 190 (Cambridge, MA: Harvard University Press, 1926), xvii.

[32] J. T. Lienhard, "*Ousia* and *Hypostasis*: The Cappadocian Settlement and the Theology of "One *Hypostasis*," in *The Trinity: An Interdisciplinary Symposium on the Trinity*, ed. S. T. Davis, D. Kendall, and G. O'Collins (Oxford: Oxford University Press, 2002), pp. 103–7.

[33] K. Anatolios, *Retrieving Nicaea: The Development and Meaning of Trinitarian Doctrine* (Grand Rapids, MI: Baker Academic, 2011), pp. 23–24.

[34] For a discussion on authorship of this epistle, found as it is also among the works of Gregory of Nyssa but addressed not to Gregory but to Peter, Bishop of Sebaste, another brother of Basil's, see n. 1 in Deferrari, *Letters 1—58*, p. 197; S. M. Hildebrand, *The Trinitarian Theology of Basil of Caesarea: A Synthesis of Greek Thought and Biblical Truth* (Washington, DC: The Catholic University of America Press, 2006), p. 47; Behr, *Nicene Faith*, 2:415. For the purpose of this study, the question of whether the epistle was written by Basil or his brother Gregory is of no critical significance given that the intent is to delineate major perspectives of the concept of the divine being and the view of the latter on the same subject will also be examined. Suffice it to say that the categorization of this epistle under the works of Basil is simply a matter of convenience, and that whether the writing is regarded as Basil's or Gregory's does not impinge upon the strength of the larger argument that the Cappadocian Fathers conceptualize the being of God as abstract quality rather than concrete personal reality.

outline his understanding of the different meanings of substance and personhood to help his brother gain a proper grasp of the subject so that he might not fall into the error of those who conceive of three substances or one person in the Trinity, wrongly believing that there is no real distinction between the concepts of substance and personhood.[35]

Basil proceeds to provide analogies from the human world of substance and personhood as applied to the Trinity, comparing the divine substance to the idea of human as quality, as used, properly, in the phrase 'Peter erred because he was only human' and, only derivatively, in 'the human (or, the one who bears human nature, or, the instantiation of human nature) took bread and ate'.[36] As for the concept of personhood, already anticipated, it points to the specific instantiation of a particular nature.[37]

In addition, according to Basil, human persons are united in being of the same essence.[38] He concludes with the observation that while the concept of personhood implies a shared nature or substance possessed by the person or persons in question, the reverse is not true; that is to say, the concept of substance does not point to any particular person.[39] These passages would be passed over without further comment were it not for the fact that the above interpretation of 'nature' and the concomitant example of the 'man' or human has been disputed by Johannes Zachhuber in favor of a view of 'nature' as an entirety of related things, and of the term 'man' as denoting all human beings.[40]

According to Richard Cross, Zachhuber posits that the writer of *Ep.* 38 distinguishes between *ousia*, which he takes as referring to nature or essence, and *phusis*, which he takes to signify an entirety of related objects.[41] It may be preferable, Cross thinks, not to introduce such a division of meaning.[42] Zachhuber's exegesis of two sections of the text as Cross presents it fails to make a convincing case, given that it appears to ignore significant elements determinant of meaning in the respective literary contexts. Consider the citation of *Ep.* 38.3 by Zachhuber in his translation where the writer speaks about

---

[35] Basil of Caesarea, *Ep.* 38.1 (Deferrari, LCL), corresponding to LCL 190:197; LCL uses the Benedictine arrangement of Basil's letters.

[36] Basil of Caesarea, *Ep.* 38.2, corresponding to LCL 190:197, 199.

[37] Ibid.

[38] Ibid.

[39] Basil of Caesarea, *Ep.* 38.3, corresponding to LCL 190:201.

[40] R. Cross, 'Gregory of Nyssa on Universals', in *VC* 56, no. 4 (2002), p. 387. *ATLA Religion Database with ATLASerials*, EBSCO*host* (accessed August 17, 2015).

[41] Ibid.

[42] Ibid., pp. 389–90.

the concept of 'man' as vague, signifying only 'nature', and incapable of reference to a specific instantiation.[43]

Taken on their own, the significations of 'nature' and 'man' are indeed ambiguous, as Cross concedes.[44] Yet, observe the difference that the inclusion of the next line makes to the meaning of the passage in which the writer employs 'nature' in the sense of that which is found in an individual.[45] If one were to insist on understanding human 'nature' in this setting as the sum total of all human beings, the example would collapse. Better sense is made by adhering to the idea of 'nature' as substance.

Moreover, Zachhuber's argument in this particular instance lacks support for coherence. If, indeed, as he contends, in the example of the writer, which Zachhuber cites,[46] the speaker has a clear referent in mind when he calls out 'man' while standing before a number of people and looking at them in such a way that and in such a setting where none of those individuals can be absolutely sure whether they are being addressed, given that these same persons by the word 'man' understand the same referent as the speaker, why should there be any need for further specification?

On the assumption that the speaker by calling out 'man' really meant 'humankind' or 'the human race' rather than 'human nature' and by extension, 'human individual', why would the individuals in his sight imagine that he might be addressing any one of them; that is, excepting a situation whereby they misunderstood him or the meaning of 'man' as 'the human race' can lead to its use as 'human individual'[47]? Accordingly, the writer of the epistle probably does not by 'man' and 'nature' in the passage in question refer to the entirety of the human race, as Zachhuber asserts, but rather to the human substance.

The second citation to be examined is from *Ep.* 38.2. Here the writer notes that the common quality encompasses all its related objects.[48] Again, there is uncertainty, until

---

[43] J. Zachhuber, *Human Nature in Gregory of Nyssa: Philosophical Background and Theological Significance* (Boston: Brill, 2014), p. 67.

[44] Cross, 'Gregory of Nyssa', p. 392.

[45] Deferrari, LCL.

[46] Zachhuber, *Human Nature in Gregory of Nyssa*, p. 67.

[47] An example of a highly metaphorical and philosophical use of a term, considering that it is easier, it would seem, to accept a derivative use of 'human nature' as 'human individual', since the individual indeed in a real sense possesses human nature, than of 'the human race' as 'human individual', since the individual does not really possess the human race; on the contrary, the reverse is true: the human race 'possesses' or contains the individual.

[48] Cross, 'Gregory of Nyssa', p. 393.

one is apprised of the immediately preceding lines whereby the idea of 'man' is applied in the setting of a bearer of a specific nature.[49]

The context demonstrates that the author has in mind not an understanding of human 'nature' as the entire human population, a supposition which would yield an unlikely rendering of a line from the same passage which suggests that an individual may be called by the name of the entire human race. Once more, an apprehension of human 'nature' as substance would resolve logical complication.[50]

Going on to specifics, in *Ep*. 38.4 Basil highlights being boundless, without origin and beyond comprehension as some elements of the substance common to all the divine persons.[51] Concerning that which is peculiar to the persons, he highlights the quality of having not been begotten in the case of the Father, and that of having been begotten in the case of the Son.[52] Basil takes great pains, with the use of the phenomenon of the rainbow, to explain how the divine persons, considered each in himself, do not manifest any difference or distinctiveness, much as it is impossible to tell where one hue of a rainbow ends and another begins when a person studies that hue in great detail; yet, the same persons, considered as a group, show forth the uniqueness of each much as the different and distinct shades of the rainbow may be perceived from a distance.

Thus, again, in seeing one divine person, one sees the other two as well; in Basil's analogy, it is like a person who pulls one end (the Spirit or Son) of a chain; in so doing, one pulls the other end (the Father and Son or Spirit) as well.[53] Unity and distinctiveness complement one another in the Godhead because that which is unique to each divine person is not a matter of the possession or lack of an absolute quality or substance, but simply one of relationship to the other persons.[54]

Consubstantiality and the concept of substance figure prominently in Basil's letter to his brother Gregory examined above. Although much of the discourse appears to be centered on arriving at a fuller understanding of personhood, as seen in the attempts from the outset to define the connotation and sense of substance and personhood, the overall thrust of the correspondence is that the divine persons are of one and the same substance. Not a digression on the part of the author, this is entirely understandable in

---

[49] Deferrari, LCL.

[50] For an argument in favor of a reading of 'nature' and 'man' in *Ep. 38* as substance from historical-philosophical context, one is referred to Cross, 'Gregory of Nyssa', esp. pp. 372–94.

[51] Basil of Caesarea, *Ep*. 38.4, corresponding to LCL 190:209.

[52] Basil of Caesarea, *Ep*. 38.7, corresponding to LCL 190:223.

[53] Basil of Caesarea, *Ep*. 38.4, corresponding to LCL 190:209, 211.

[54] Basil of Caesarea, *Ep*. 38.8, corresponding to LCL 190:227.

light of the fact that it was probably easier for people in his time to accept ontological difference between the Father, Son and Holy Spirit, rather than identity of essence.

Indeed, Basil seems to show this to be the case by the way in which he chooses to address an argument against the full ontological status of the personhood of the Son,[55] revealing that the influence of the followers of Aetius and Eunomius,[56] who taught that the Father and Son were ontologically unlike but did not dispute the kind of similarity between the two in scripture which, so Eunomius thinks, does not include ontological similarity but involves another kind of similarity,[57] was sufficiently significant and threatening to justify his writing specifically to Gregory of Nyssa concerning the matter as part of an endeavor to keep the latter from falling into theological error or heresy.[58] In addition, that a discussion of substance forms an important portion of an exploration of personhood is consistent with Basil's view that personhood constitutes a concretization of substance or common or shared nature.[59] Such a consideration sheds light on the relationship Basil sees between the worship of God and divine being and personhood, a topic which was previously discussed.[60]

Divine substance is central to the adoration of God without implying that the impersonal is being worshipped because the person is comprised of the substance of which the same is made as well as his peculiar features. The being and nature of the divine persons is core in religious devotion because even as it is something abstract and fundamental to the person, it is indirectly visible to other beings, manifested to the same in the

---

[55] Basil of Caesarea, *Ep.* 38.6–8, corresponding to LCL 190:219, 221, 223, 225, 227; Basil devotes thirty percent of the length of his epistle to respond to this query revolving around the understanding of the scriptural view of the personhood of the Son.

[56] For a discussion of the propriety and meanings of terms used to refer to the followers of Aetius and Eunomius, consult L. Ayres, *Nicaea and Its Legacy: An Approach to Fourth-Century Trinitarian Theology* (Oxford: Oxford University Press, 2006), pp. 144–45.

[57] Eunomius of Cyzicus, *Apol.* 1.22 (Vaggione, OECT).

[58] Consider the facts that Basil had in the decade in which the correspondence was written just issued a response to an apology, so called, of Eunomius, and that Aetius and Eunomius were around this time actively and systematically propagating their version of the doctrine of God. See R. P. Vaggione, *Eunomius: The Extant Works*, OECT (Oxford: Oxford University Press, 1987), pp. 5–6; Ayres, *Nicaea*, p. 146.

[59] Basil of Caesarea, *Ep.* 38.3 (Deferrari, LCL), corresponding to LCL 190:201.

[60] Concerning Basil of Caesarea *Spir.* 18.45. Both the thirty-eighth epistle and *On the Holy Spirit* were written within three to six years of one another. See n. 1 in Deferrari, *Letters 1—58*, p. 197; S. Hildebrand, *On the Holy Spirit*, PPS 42 (Yonkers, NY: St. Vladimir's Seminary Press, 2011), p. 22.

form of behavior and actions. In contrast, apart from the incarnation the seats of consciousness of the Father, Son, and Holy Spirit are indiscernible.[61]

Thence, it is the divine nature of the persons rather than their personhood as a whole, which includes their seats of consciousness, that inspires worship of the persons, but that worship is directed towards the whole person, encompassing both nature and seat of consciousness.

---

[61] Jürgen Moltmann's observation that the Father is Father only of the Son adds coherence to the Basilian or Gregorian insistence that the hypostases can only be differentiated internally. The point is that the names Father, Son, and Holy Spirit define the relationships between them. J. Moltmann, *The Trinity and the Kingdom: The Doctrine of God*, trans. M. Kohl (Minneapolis, MN: Fortress Press, 1993), pp. 162–63, 183.

Chapter 2

Basil of Caesarea, B

Epistula 214

Basil does not merely conceive of the divine being in the category of nature; he also thinks of being in terms of orientation and action, as when, in a letter to a Count Terentius, he identifies goodness as an element of the being of the divine persons. Since goodness cannot exist simply as a part of being, without existing also in the dimensions of purpose and action, to identify goodness as an element of the divine being is to assert that the meaning of the concept of divine being embraces makeup, orientation and action. In the same passage he takes up the subject of the relation between substance and personhood.[1]

Writing against the background of the infiltration into the church of modalistic thinking of the Trinity, which posits that there is only one person in the godhead rather than three so that there is no real distinction between the persons since there is but one divine person, Basil defends the scriptural idea that the personhood of the Trinity is as real as the being of the same. This former false notion, he seems to contend, arises from a misinterpretation of the concept of divine personhood as synonymous in meaning with that of divine substance or being, necessitating a clarification of the significations of the two concepts.

---

[1] Basil of Caesarea, *Ep.* 214.4 (Deferrari, LCL), corresponding to LCL 243:235.

According to Basil, to revisit his important point, the concept of substance points to the nature of something whereas that of personhood points to the individual entity itself. By speaking of taking part in (μετέχω) as the nature of the relationship of something to its being, and subsistence (εἰμί) as that of something to its peculiar characteristics, which may be defined in terms of self-identity, he makes clear that what is particular is more fundamental to an entity than that which is general, and that, by implication, that which is general is less fundamental to an entity than that which is particular.

For this reason, the suggestion must be rejected which Holmes makes in support of his perspective that the Cappadocian Fathers did not hold to a doctrine in which the divine persons have distinct centers of consciousness.[2] Holmes' formulation of that which is of the divine essence does not accord with Basil's concept of the substance of God, which incorporates abstract qualities like rationality rather than concrete realities like the mind of God as opposed to the mind of someone else.

Accordingly, there is in principle no reason to reject the notion of the divine persons as having individual centers of consciousness as posited by the Cappadocians. In fact, it is crucial to their theology of the divine being. If the being of God is defined as the qualitatively but not numerically identical substance of the three divine persons, the full reality of God subsists in each of the persons. Thus, deity as abstract quality is entirely concretized as much in the Father, as in the Son, and as in the Holy Spirit, and there is no concrete divine reality beyond them because the divine substance cannot exist on its own, but only in the three divine persons. On this premise, the personal dimension of God must be situated in each of the divine persons, since they are ontologically equal, and there is nothing ontologically greater than any one of them, and, above all, the fullness of the divine being, which is personal, subsists in each of them.

In what sense, however, might one speak of God as personal? Is there an inherent error in understanding God *qua* personal as a being? Fiddes is of the opinion that God should not be ranked with created entities as merely a being among others.[3] Embedded in this reasoning seem to be the assumptions that any kind of ontological resemblance between the Creator and his creatures is unworthy of the former and detracts from his

---

[2] S. R. Holmes, 'Classical Trinity: Evangelical Perspective', in *Two Views on the Doctrine of the Trinity*, ed. J. S. Sexton and S. N. Gundry (Grand Rapids, MI: Zondervan, 2014), p. 38. This disagreement is shared, though without the same argumentation, by P. S. Fiddes in 'Relational Trinity: Radical Perspective', in *Two Views on the Doctrine of the Trinity*, ed. J. S. Sexton and S. N. Gundry, Counterpoints (Grand Rapids, MI: Zondervan, 2014), pp. 164–65.

[3] Ibid., p. 174.

uniqueness, and that created things have an independent existence which permits their comparison with an independently existing Creator.

Yet it is by no means the case that to regard God as a being in a way that superficially recalls created entities prejudices his deity. This is because even if both deity and creature are described using the same term, the significations of each application are quite disparate. In regard to the creaturely order, the senses of finiteness and contingency are retained. When speaking of God, however, the word comes to denote what is by nature boundless and without origin.

Is there any justification, then, in maintaining use of the term to signify God as well as creature? The answer must be given in the positive, considering that according to biblical witness which the Cappadocians are quite unlikely to have ignored, the Creator relates with his human creatures. As much as God is the source of all existence, including those with whom he deals, he encounters and confronts them as a reality external to them, a reality which is capable of knowing, perceiving, feeling, desiring, willing, relating, speaking and acting in a coherent and organized fashion in accordance to his character and purpose.

If it continues to be doubted whether the Cappadocian Fathers did in fact interpret the biblical testimony as shown, it might be underscored that like all Christians in their day they embraced the basic confession of God as Creator.[4] Here is a momentous piece of evidence that reveals the mind of the ancient fathers, for if they believed in God as the Creator of the universe, in the words of the Nicene Creed, surely they by implication believed also in God as a cognitive, conative and competent entity, for the creative act presupposes not just ability, but also the will to accomplish a plan and design for an orderly cosmos, which in turn presupposes supreme rationality, thereby qualifying God in the Old Testament to be considered as a person today.[5]

Might not the created order be the mere result of the unfolding of a 'world mind', a non-living or living but insentient being? If so, the rationality of this 'mind' would have to be accounted for. However, this rationality has no source if the 'world mind' is the ultimate reality since it is insentient. On the other hand, if a Creator is posited, the ra-

---

[4] E.g. Basil of Caesarea, *Spir.* 16.38, Gregory of Nazianzus, *Or.* 40.45, Gregory of Nyssa, *Eun.* 1.26. A convenient compilation of texts on the topic is afforded by G. L. Bray, ed., *We Believe in One God*, ACD 1 (Downers Grove, IL: IVP Academic, 2009), in the relevant section.

[5] According to a definition by William Alston in S. Coakley, "'Persons' in the 'Social' Doctrine of the Trinity: A Critique of Current Analytic Discussion', in *The Trinity: An Interdisciplinary Symposium on the Trinity*, ed. S. T. Davis, D. Kendall, and G. O'Collins (Oxford: Oxford University Press, 2002), p. 130, n. 26.

tionality is explained by his unchanging plan, which is in accordance with his wisdom and goodness, of which he is the essence. Might the divine persons be automatons? If this is postulated, there would need to be an external source of will, but the divine persons are the ultimate principle in Cappadocian theology. Therefore the divine persons are not automatons. As such, the Cappadocians did not hold to a view of God as an automaton, but as having a personality, on which the rest of the biblical witness elaborates.

In this way, God as ultimate being is the ground from which flowers grow, but as being among other beings, unique in being ontologically independent, he is also a flower, which other flowers are able to face.[6] Therefore God may be understood as personal in the sense of being a cognitive, conative, affective, relational, and competent entity. In short, he is a socio-psychological entity. For the Cappadocians, 'God' is either an alternate name for one of the persons, such as the Father,[7] or a term that signifies the divine being or substance. On their account, then, the divine persons constitute socio-psychological entities.

Does this idea militate against the simplicity of God? Not if simplicity is understood as being of the nature of the divine being rather than of the number of the bearers of the divine being. The substance of God is indeed simple and non-composite. It cannot be divided into smaller parts because it does not possess any constituent parts. Although there is multiplicity in the divine essence, which is to be conceived at all times as quality, this is multiplicity of dimension and not multiplicity of quantity.

To use an example from objects commonly observed, the divine essence is to the divine person what, say, the color red, smoothness of texture, and durability of material is to a sofa. Here are three different ideas pertaining to the sofa, but these are qualitative ideas, and by their very nature irreducible. In other words, in horizontal terms, it is not possible to determine which one of the three ideas is least dispensable and more essential in an effort to reduce the 'essence' of the sofa to a simpler state with two aspects or

---

[6] This twofold understanding of the divine being seems to fit the thesis of Martin Heidegger in 'The Onto-Theo-Logical Constitution of Metaphysics', in *Identity and Difference*, trans. J. Stambaugh (Chicago: The University of Chicago Press, 2002), pp. 42–76, esp. 70–71. As ground of all reality, the philosophical concept of 'Being' is of an abstract, impersonal ultimate reality which explains and forms the being of created entities on the one hand, and is expressed and realized only in the entirety of its concrete instantiations, on the other. Yet, conceived as the highest being of all beings, Being is seen as the ultimate and efficient cause of all that derives being from it. In all of this, Heidegger does not propose a dichotomy between the two notions and perspectives, as seen in p. 58. For this reason, his comment in p. 72 concerning how Being, purely philosophically conceived as ground of all reality, cannot receive worship, has to be read as an attempt to contrast the two views, which paradoxically concern a single referent rather than two separate ones.

[7] Basil of Caesarea, *Spir.* 18.44 (Hildebrand, PPS).

just one. What about the degree of redness or smoothness or durability? Surely that can be reduced to 'lower' states or raised to higher ones?

This is where the human analogy breaks down. First, it must be borne in mind that with the perfect divine being, there are no degrees of being to which it may logically be relegated; this was the crucial insight of St. Basil.[8] A perfect being, by definition, is not simply a substance that surpasses all others in greatness of virtue, as if it were the result of an extremely long evolution from simplicity to complexity. No, a perfect being as Christians understand it is perfect in its essence. Consequently, it is the source, in a purely ontological sense, in all creation of the dimensions of which it is perfection. As uncreated and unchanging source, not coming into existence or arising through gradual development, it is simple and not composed of parts. One plainly cannot speak of degrees of being in regard to the source of being; to do so is tantamount to asking how much water there is contained in the source of water that flows through an open hose, thinking that it is comparable to a bucket or some other container.

Returning to the example of the red, smooth, and durable sofa, if divine essence were to divine person what the number of sofas was to a sofa, it would be possible to reduce the 'essence' from three to one by removing two sofas. This, however, is not the case, and so the divine essence is non-composite and simple even as it is multiple in facet or dimension; as a matter of fact, it is simple by definition, being a qualitative rather than quantitative factor from which all creaturely being is produced.

Dissimilar to any created object, the doctrine of divine simplicity requires that the divine being not merely possess properties without which it could still be imagined.[9] Equating the divine being with the attributes commonly ascribed to it has resulted in the inconvenient quandary of having to account for the linguistic and logical ramifications of so doing; for instance, if God is said to be identical to his love and to his power, the implication seems to be that love and power are identical qualities.[10]

As Andrew Radde-Gallwitz has lucidly demonstrated, an alternate route was charted by the genius of Basil of Caesarea and Gregory of Nyssa who salvaged the divine attributes from complete irrelevance in the hands of Eunomius, who alleged that the di-

---

[8] Holmes, 'Classical Trinity: Evangelical Perspective', pp. 35–36.

[9] P. Sanlon, *Simply God: Recovering the Classical Trinity* (Nottingham, England: Inter-Varsity, 2014), pp. 59–61. For a survey of different perspectives on the doctrine of divine simplicity, consult T. H. McCall, 'Trinity Doctrine, Plain and Simple', in *Advancing Trinitarian Theology: Explorations in Constructive Dogmatics*, ed. O. D. Crisp and F. Sanders, Los Angeles Theology Conference (Grand Rapids, MI: Zondervan, 2014), pp. 42–59, esp. 54–59.

[10] Ibid., p. 62.

vine essence, that is to say, the defining quality of God, could be comprehended by human beings and entirely expressed by a term signifying the state of not having been produced, and from logical difficulty by proposing that God's attributes are to be understood as not defining the divine essence but nonetheless indispensable to the divine being.[11]

The idea of necessary divine features obviates the need to choose between claiming the possibility of understanding of the divine essence, and absolute agnosticism about the divine being by differentiating between a definitive and exhaustive knowledge of God, and a certain but non-definitive knowledge of the divine being by means of a subtle distinction between the defining quality of God and the divine being in itself.[12] Using this scheme, one may posit the divine being as possessing multiple indispensable characteristics without having thereby to sacrifice the notion of a divine simplicity.

Interestingly, in the theology of Gregory of Nyssa, the latter requires the former, as Radde-Gallwitz has shown. This is due to the fact that the highest moral qualities require one another.[13] A little earlier, he provides a translation of Gregory's exposition of the mutual entailment of perfect human virtues.[14] Concerning the divine being, the conflict is not with the multiplicity of these inseparable moral qualities, Radde-Gallwitz expresses, but lack of corruption by the presence of their contraries, which is the meaning of simplicity as applied to the divine being in Gregory's thought.[15] In the final analysis, the antithesis of divine simplicity is not multiplicity *per se* but complexity.

Another, complementary, way out of the logical dilemma posited earlier concerning equating God with his attributes is to emphasize that difficulty attends the notion of equating God with his attributes fundamentally because while he is not any less than the essence of his attributes, he is also more than them. The concepts of love or power or any other divine attribute for that matter are not adequate to express the essence of God. To posit God as, say, love in essence, is really quite reductionist. God is love, but the love which he is has a dimension of justice, which is often so far from the human notion of the concept that to speak alone of love as defining an infinitely small part of the divine essence easily tends toward misunderstanding.

---

[11] A. Radde-Gallwitz, *Basil of Caesarea, Gregory of Nyssa, and the Transformation of Divine Simplicity*, OECS (Oxford: Oxford University Press, 2009). See 'Note to the Reader', the introduction, and chs. 6 and 7, esp. pp. 184, 200, 202.

[12] Ibid., 'Note to Reader' and the introduction.

[13] Ibid., p. 212.

[14] Ibid., p. 211, translated from *Catech.* 20.

[15] Ibid., p. 212.

Christians can affirm that God is love even in light of his vengeance against his enemies, for in his vengeance he reveals his justice and fairness; that is, himself; because of this, God benefits even his enemies in that he reveals himself to them, and if the experience of divine self-disclosure is the greatest good, it must be concluded that God does the greatest good, yes, to his enemies, and that, by implication, he displays love toward them even amid, indeed, through judgment. One would expect that such a notion of divine love would be alien and even unpalatable to modern and postmodern sensibility. As such, there is no real error in proclaiming love, or any other divine attribute, as defining an infinitely small part of the divine essence, but those ideas have to be almost completely rehabilitated to speak truly of God.

Before leaving the subject, in light of extensive discussion concerning the source and origin of the self-awareness of the divine persons, it may be helpful to propose that the idea of necessary divine features furnishes a solution.[16] The problem of how three divine persons with exactly the same knowledge, including that of one another's experiences, may maintain an accurate self-awareness has been broached. There is a tendency to conceive of divine self-awareness as dependent, like human self-awareness, on memory.[17] This need not be thought of as the sole approach. As a matter of fact, such a proposition is theological unviable and inadvisable, considering that memory entails the passing of time, yet the divine persons in their eternity do not experience the passage of time.

It may not be necessary to commit to a view of divine self-awareness as a function of memory, as having a source or origin. If this is challenged, one's attention is directed to how in human beings, both self-awareness and moral goodness are derivative factors, with the former rooted in memory of past experiences, and the latter, in God, who alone is good (Luke 18:19). There is little dispute, at least among evangelical theologians, regarding the possibility and favorability of thinking of the moral goodness of God as independent. Why, then, should anyone object to the idea of the independence of the self-awareness of the divine persons? In the same way that the divine persons 'begin', that is to say, are always and only conceived, with mutually agreed commitments to their respective roles as Father, Son, and Holy Spirit, so they possess distinctive forms of self-awareness, by which they are able to distinguish between self and the other two divine persons.

---

[16] This is to apply Radde-Gallwitz's thesis in a new context and thereby go beyond it by building upon it.

[17] D. Brown, *The Divine Trinity* (La Salle, IL: Open Court, 1985), pp. 284–89, esp. 289.

These forms of self-awareness, like the self-identities, are unique to each divine person; nevertheless, they are indispensable traits, albeit not ones that are common to the divine being.[18] As Holmes has noted, St. Augustine observes that the relationships denoted by the names of the divine persons, and the names themselves while not having to do with the divine essence nonetheless signify that which is unchangeable.[19]

It might be useful to observe that when Gregory of Nazianzus or Augustine seem to equate the names of the divine persons with the idea of relationship,[20] they are using the words 'Father', 'Son', and 'Holy Spirit' not in the sense of the actual entities who bear those names but of the roles they have and which their names signify, much as, for instance, the word 'President' might refer either to the office, perhaps, of the executive head of a company or to the bearer of that office. As an example of a sentence utilizing the former signification, one might suggest 'after undergoing a radical reshuffling, that company is looking to fill three key positions: President, Vice-President (Operations), and Communications Director'. An instance of use of the latter signification can be found in 'the President is taking his breakfast'.

With a view of the divine persons as three cognitive and conative entities, is there no safeguard against the degeneration of the Godhead into a polytheistic triad characterized by 'gods' with different agendas? This possibility is precluded on the basis of the implications of the divine attributes as traditionally understood. Let us begin with the divine persons as perfectly wise. Might there be among three perfectly wise divine persons competing or at least different visions of a perfect universe?

Add to the discussion the fact that the divine persons are also omnipotent and sovereign, so that their will[21] is always performed, and it is impossible to avoid the conclusion that there is but one perfect vision of the cosmos, since of all possibilities of the

---

[18] In Gregory Nazianzen's thought, McGuckin highlights in "Perceiving Light from Light in Light' (*Oration* 31.3): The Trinitarian Theology of Saint Gregory the Theologian', in *GOTR* 39, no. 1 (1994), pp. 10, 29; *ATLA Religion Database with ATLASerials*, EBSCO*host* (accessed August 13, 2015), the personal properties peculiar to each divine person, those of being without origin (to the Father), generated (to the Son), and proceeding (to the Holy Spirit) constitute their indispensable characteristics.

[19] Augustine of Hippo, *Trin.* 5.6 (Hill, WSA; cited in Holmes, 'Classical Trinity: Evangelical Perspective', p. 30).

[20] Ibid. and Gregory of Nazianzus, *Or.* 29.16 (Wickham, PPS; cited in Holmes, 'Classical Trinity: Evangelical Perspective', pp. 29–30).

[21] Whether it be the things which they abominate but purposefully permit or those in which they are directly and beatifically involved.

ultimate future, only one can materialize. That which materializes is necessarily the will of each of the divine persons, seeing that they are perfectly sovereign.

If the ultimate future that transpired were not to be the will of any of the divine persons, the divine person in question would not thereby be omnipotent and sovereign, because the will of the divine person is not carried out, and the definition of divine sovereignty is that one's will is always performed. However, it is not possible for any divine person to be anything less than omnipotent and sovereign. Accordingly, the ultimate future that will transpire will be the will of each divine person. This implies that perfect wisdom is associated with one single plan for the universe, and that the divine persons, while having distinct centers of consciousness, being perfectly wise are united in their purpose.

This is not to imply that Basil or the other Cappadocians saw an exact correspondence between divine and human persons, even if they may on occasion draw a loose analogy between them.[22] A glaring distinction lies in how with human beings, fallen or not, each has a slightly different substance which results in a differing approach to problems, set of interests, personality, and physical appearance, albeit human persons are sufficiently close to one another to be classed in a common category.[23]

In the case of the divine being, there is but one substance, exactly one kind of essence.[24] This is a logical necessity that attends the doctrine of the indivisibility of divine action. It would be impossible for entities with different inclinations to agree all the time, and equally impossible for those with identical inclinations to disagree. Indeed, Gregory

---

[22] Therefore, on the one hand, the Cappadocian Fathers are said by writers like William Lane Craig in 'Toward a Tenable Social Trinitarianism', in *Philosophical and Theological Essays on the Trinity*, ed. T. McCall and M. C. Rea (Oxford: Oxford University Press, 2009), p. 89, to draw such a comparison and yet a writer like McGuckin in 'Perceiving Light from Light in Light', pp. 19–25, has demonstrated from the theology of Gregory of Nazianzus the error of those who take the analogy between the divine persons and human beings in an overly literal manner because such an analogy ultimately fails to do justice to the identity of the being of the divine persons. Kathryn Tanner alludes to the same point in *Jesus, Humanity and the Trinity: A Brief Systematic Theology*, Scottish Journal of Theology: Current Issues in Theology (Edinburgh: T&T Clark, 2001), p. 38 and n. 11 on the same page. Tanner however is mistaken in ascribing to the Cappadocians a view of the three divine persons as having an essence that is numerically one rather than simply qualitatively identical. This is because the Cappadocian concept of the divine being is as nature, or quality, which is the burden of this study to show and which is hopefully compellingly demonstrated; in the thought of the Cappadocian Fathers, the idea of the divine being points not to the concrete entity, of which it may be said that it is numerically one, but to the abstract, of which no such suggestion may be made.

[23] See Gregory of Nazianzus, *Or.* 31.15 (Wickham, PPS).

[24] McGuckin, 'Perceiving Light from Light in Light', p. 25.

of Nyssa argues from the inseparability of divine operations that there is but one substance or nature,[25] suggesting that human persons have different substances and natures in light of how their actions differ. Although the divine persons do function at separate levels of action, this is more a matter of an eternal mutual agreement and adherence to roles in a divine hierarchy than one of personal preference. Consequently, in the theology of the Cappadocian Fathers, the divine persons have a qualitatively identical substance that is the divine being, whereas in the realm of humanity, individuals differ as much as resemble one another in their substances.

Divine being and the oneness of God is, then, not to be perceived so much in a personal sense as an individual divine entity, but an abstract and qualitative one as the attributes or makeup, orientation and action of three divine entities.[26]

There is a last remark to be made concerning the passage in question: In associating the power of holiness as a distinctive characteristic with the Holy Spirit, and not with the Father or the Son, Basil is not claiming that the Holy Spirit has a monopoly on power and holiness or the power of holiness or power that is holy, of which the other two divine persons are deprived. To make such a contention would be to flatly contradict the teaching of Scripture that holiness, power and divinity are inseparable,[27] and, to imply that the Father and Son do not fully share in the divine being to the extent that they do not possess divine holiness and power. It is better to suppose that in linking the power of holiness uniquely with the Holy Spirit Basil was simply using a shorthand to denote the special self-identity of the Holy Spirit.

Epistula 236

In his epistle to Amphilochius, the one numbered two hundred and thirty-sixth, in endeavoring to provide a proper reading of a passage in the Gospel of Mark which has been construed by his opponents as establishing that at least the earthly Christ was not all-knowing, Basil adds omniscience to the general attributes of the divine persons.[28]

---

[25] Gregory of Nyssa, *Sanct. Trin.* GNO 3.1:10.14–13.21 (Wilson, *NPNF*² 5: 328-29).

[26] Basil of Caesarea, *Ep.* 214.4 (Deferrari, LCL), corresponding to LCL 243:235.

[27] For instance, in Rev. 4 St. John reported a scene in heaven to which he was transported in which four living creatures worshipped the Father by declaring that He is holy, and almighty or omnipotent.

[28] Basil of Caesarea, *Ep.* 236.2 (Deferrari, LCL), corresponding to LCL 243:395.

Further on in his letter in which he addresses several subjects, Basil discourses on the distinctive meanings of the concepts of substance and personhood.[29]

Considering that much attention has already been given to Basil's understanding of substance as generic and person as particular, there is little need to belabor the point, except to highlight that the use of a word signifying a life-containing entity made by God is in the sense of the nature and makeup shared by all the entities that are classed under that general category.[30] In this way, the following reference to and illustration from the concept of a specific human individual finds a framework in which it can fit neatly, with the ideas of substance and personhood expressing different dimensions: the former, the characteristics or attributes, and the latter, the specific entity itself with its sense of self-identity.

The more significant insight to be gleaned from the passage cited above must be the middle portion in which Basil effectively and conclusively defines the divine persons as having two inseparable dimensions: first, the substance, which is the set of attributes and qualities common to the divine persons, to the members of the godhead; and, second, personhood, designating the divine persons themselves, those persons which possess the qualities belonging to the members of the godhead and to divinity.

In regard to the reason Basil speaks of a need to join personhood to substance, this is to be found in the fact that the epistle in question was written not long after that to Count Terentius, which has already been reviewed, and in which the Cappadocian father made a valiant effort to persuade his addressee not to be deceived by the arguments of the modalists so as to shift his support away from Basil to them. Something of the frightening ability of his opponents to turn the tide to their favor is captured and conveyed in his urgent words to the official.[31] The situation in which the letter to Amphilochius was written, which is presently being examined, is the same.

Modalism continued to represent a threat to the church, the variant doctrinal instruction being that the concept of divine personhood has the same meaning as that of divine substance. This occasioned a firm and uncompromising response on the part of Basil, who gave the church the terminology to speak of the triune nature of God by defining the theological meaning of the concept of personhood, which then became the basis on which to arrive at a timeless and still compelling vision of the deity, as a triad or group of ontologically equal and equally divine persons, equal in majesty, goodness, ho-

---

[29] Basil of Caesarea, *Ep.* 236.6, corresponding to LCL 243:401, 403, 405.
[30] See Brown, *Divine Trinity*, p. 276.
[31] Basil of Caesarea, *Ep.* 214.4, corresponding to LCL 190:235, 237.

liness, wisdom, power and glory, a vision in which the concept of being describes rather than denotes the divine.[32]

Behr makes a contrary claim in his analysis of *Ep.* 38, which he attributes to Gregory of Nyssa, in contending that the divine being signifies the Father. He does not, however, appear to make a convincing argument for his assertion that Basil, Gregory Nazianzen, and Gregory Nyssen conceive of the oneness of God chiefly in terms of the Father. In the case of Gregory Nyssen, he derives the idea of a monarchy of the Father from an unusual translation of a preposition-noun combination, and tortuous interpretation of the same: ἐπὶ πάντων to express a certain superiority of the Father in relation to the Son and Holy Spirit.[33]

In the final analysis, there is good warrant for maintaining that Basil of Caesarea holds a view of the divine being as the identical substance, will, purpose, and action of the Father, the Son, and the Holy Spirit.

---

[32] See F. Dünzl, *A Brief History of the Doctrine of the Trinity in the Early Church*, trans. J. Bowden (London: T&T Clark, 2007), pp. 106–7.

[33] See Behr in *The Nicene Faith*, vol. 2 of *The Formation of Christian Theology* (Crestwood, NY: St. Vladimir's Seminary Press, 2004), 2:419–20. In the case of Basil, see this writer's commentary on *Spir.* 18.44–45. In the case of Gregory Nazianzen, see this writer's commentary on *Or.* 29.2.

Chapter 3

Gregory of Nazianzus

Oratio 29

Christened 'The Theologian', Gregory Nazianzen spoke, in his famed theological orations, of God not so much as single concrete being but as substance, will, purpose, and action, common to the divine persons.[1]

That Gregory in his third theological oration defines Christian belief in a sole God in terms of governance[2] of the affairs of the universe by persons who are numerically three yet conduct the business of rule without any difference or diversity in stance among them or, indeed, any action that is not performed by all three at one and the same time, is instructive.

The point being made is that the oneness of God has to do not just with divine capacities, but also and equally with internal disposition, orientation, and even external action. After all, to redefine the being of God as a state of continuous action in perfectly identical rule is to embrace, yes, the abilities of the divine persons, but as well, their character, which determines one's value system and therefore direction or philosophy of

---

[1] Gregory of Nazianzus, *Or.* 29.2 (Wickham, PPS).

[2] John Zizioulas notes that the term μοναρχία (Gregory of Nazianzus, *Or.* 29 [PG 36:2b]) was used both to denote government by one ruler and united governance ('μοναρχ-ία, ἡ', *LSJ* 2:1143). J. D. Zizioulas, *Communion and Otherness: Further Studies in Personhood and the Church* (London: T & T Clark, 2006), p. 119.

leadership, and the actions that arise from those factors. Continuous and identical action is not possible without identity of ability, character, value system, and purpose.

This commentary differs from that offered by Behr in that the translation adopted of πρὸς τὸ ἓν τῶν ἐξ αὐτοῦ σύννευσις in *Or.* 29.2 renders πρὸς τὸ ἕν... σύννευσις as 'in reference to the unity... agreement' to make for 'agreement in reference to unity of those of it'.[3] Such a rendering is to be preferred because it fits the context better. The clause occurs as one among four characteristics listed by Nazianzen of the unity of rule by the divine persons, which John Behr notes.[4]

It is difficult to see how the fourth item, if it is taken as a reference to the closing in of the Son and Spirit on the Father, would contribute to Gregory's point that there is a unity of essence among the divine persons. Therefore, the fourth item refers to the unity of the essence shared by the Father, Son, and Holy Spirit, with which the divine persons are in accord—so that operation and nature are in complete harmony, thereby ensuring the possibility of a unified rule—and of which they are constituted, rather than to a unity centered on the Father.[5] In the same oration as the one earlier quoted, he draws an analogy between the divine persons and animals and human beings.[6]

Obviously, he was not thinking of the concept of species mentioned in the text in a modern scientific sense. To suggest so is to commit an anachronism and introduce an idea that is foreign to the literary context. Instead, Gregory was utilizing the philosophical notion of essence, as the concept of species was understood by the ancients,[7] to assert that there is a set of attributes common and unique to the three divine persons, just as to animals grouped under the same 'species', and to the human race as a whole. In the case of the divine persons, the common and exclusive set of traits being referenced may be those of their distinctive character,[8] powers, as well as the distinctive way in which they act together to govern the universe.

---

[3] 'πρός', *LSJ* 2:1496–99; 'εἷς', *PGL* 470; 'σύν-νευσις', *LSJ* 2:1719.

[4] J. Behr, *The Nicene Faith*, vol. 2 of *The Formation of Christian Theology* (Crestwood, NY: St. Vladimir's Seminary Press, 2004), 2:342–43.

[5] Cf. Ayres, *Nicaea*, pp. 216, 244–45.

[6] Gregory of Nazianzus, *Or.* 29.13.

[7] In this instance, by Aristotle. R. Audi, ed., *The Cambridge Dictionary of Philosophy*, 2nd ed. (Cambridge: Cambridge University Press, 1999), s.v. 'Aristotle'.

[8] At least in the case of the Christian God, since the Greco-Roman gods were often as immoral if not more so than humans. Could the notion of consanguinity between Greek gods and human beings be a hint of an attempt to justify the moral likeness between the two?

Gregory in his fifth theological oration describes the Trinity in a succinct statement.⁹ With an economy of words, in which ἰδιότης, referring to 'particular existences',¹⁰ may be rendered with the idea of personhood,¹¹ he captures the real issue underlying the question of how the three and the one in the Trinity may be reconciled: the one in God is abstract, pertaining to the distinctive characteristics of the divine persons which make for a monarchy, while the three is personal. He also compares the relationship between the divine substance and divine persons with that between human nature and a human being.¹²

The tension between the general and the specific in the divine persons is here explained by recourse to the concept of a shared identity. This is another trait that sets human beings apart from other creatures: they are conscious that they are human. More importantly, a bid is made to lay bare the implication of postulating that God is to be conceived as three persons with the same divine nature by giving a picture from the human world of persons who are equally human but also individuals, the indivisible existing in the divided, unity coexisting with differentiation.

Understood alongside earlier sections, there is certainly no intimation here of tritheism or claim that two of the divine persons had a beginning; this section must be read in light of the fact that it is part of Gregory's effort to demonstrate that the Holy Spirit, who is not the Son of God who shares in the nature of the Father, is nevertheless as divine as the Father and the Son. Moreover, there is a hint in the analogy of the concept of the replication of the divine substance transmitted from the Father in the Son and the Holy Spirit. Further along the way, Gregory repeats that the three divine persons are one because they are one in their makeup or nature.¹³

The words in *Or.* 31.14, πρῶτος αἰτία,¹⁴ according to their usage in the Septuagint and New Testament, refer to a preeminent thing which brings about a state.¹⁵ Yet αἰτία is also used by Aristotle, whom Alston argues provided inspiration for the development

---

⁹ Gregory of Nazianzus, *Or.* 31.9.
¹⁰ 'ἰδιότης', *LSJ* 1:818; Gregory of Nazianzus, *Or.* 31 (PG 36:9a).
¹¹ According to Wickham, Gregory uses ἰδιότης as a synonym for ὑπόστασις.
¹² Gregory of Nazianzus, *Or.* 31.11.
¹³ Gregory of Nazianzus, *Or.* 31.14.
¹⁴ Gregory of Nazianzus, *Or.* 31 (PG 36:14a).
¹⁵ 'πρῶτος, η, ον', *BDAG* 892–94; 'αἰτία, ας, ἡ', *BDAG* 31.

of the person-substance theory of Basil and Gregory of Nyssa,[16] to signify cause in four senses: *material, efficient, formal,* and *final*.[17] In this context, Gregory is using αἰτία in the sense of *material* cause, to denote the divine nature that constitutes the three persons.

The other meanings are excluded by the general understanding of the Trinity—the divine persons could not have derived their being from anything other than the substance of which they are constituted, whether a mere form, plan or purpose, for such a suggestion carries the implication that the divine persons had a beginning in time, and if the divine persons are said here to have derived their being from their substance, this is simply an oblique way of expressing that the divine persons share in the same divine nature, for it is impossible, again, that something should have existed before the divine persons, even if it be their substance—and the immediate literary context. Read in this way, the term denotes the nature or makeup of an entity.

In making the above point, the writer departs from the interpretation of Behr, who sees in the passage a reference to the monarchy of Father by relating πρῶτος αἰτία with the Father.[18] Behr's reading is unnatural for a couple of reasons: If πρῶτος αἰτία refers to the Father, Gregory Nazianzen would in effect be suggesting that the Father could be contemplated apart from the Son and Holy Spirit.

Yet, can the Father indeed be dissociated from the Son and the Holy Spirit? Does not 'Father' presuppose 'Son' and vice versa? Second, if Gregory were indeed distinguishing the Father from the other divine persons, there should be two objects for contemplation rather than three, since, in the connection that Gregory makes in this passage, that which is from something (in Behr's view, referring in the text only to the Son and Holy Spirit) cannot be numerically identical to that from which it is (the Father). More than an academic point, this is important for justifying use of the passage in question to

---

[16] W. P. Alston, 'Substance and the Trinity', in *The Trinity: An Interdisciplinary Symposium on the Trinity*, ed. S. T. Davis, D. Kendall, and G. O'Collins (Oxford: Oxford University Press, 2002), pp. 183–89.

[17] 'αἰτ-α', *LSJ* 1:44; Audi, *Cambridge Dictionary of Philosophy*, s.v. 'Aristotle'. Although Gregory uses that philosophical concept, he does not thereby imply that it sufficiently conveys truth about God's nature; nowhere do the Cappadocians suggest that the divine persons are completely described as members of a class or species, of which there may be more than three; rather, they are of the view that God exists in three persons, and by implication that there is an inextricable link between individual personhood and common substance. See K. Corrigan, 'Οὐσία and ὑπόστασις in the Trinitarian Theology of the Cappadocian Fathers: Basil and Gregory of Nyssa', *ZAC* 12 (2008), p. 122; *ATLA Religion Database with ATLASerials*, EBSCO*host* (accessed February 28, 2015).

[18] Behr, *Nicene Faith*, 2:364–65; for another alternative reading, see R. Letham, *The Holy Trinity: In Scripture, History, Theology, and Worship* (Phillipsburg, NJ: P&R, 2004), pp. 162–63.

demonstrate the concept of the divine being of Gregory of Nazianzus as substance, will, purpose, and action, which unites the three divine persons.

This is not to imply that Gregory does not understand the Father as being cause and origin, relationally, within the Trinity; he clearly does. In this regard, there are at least two senses to Gregory's concept of αἰτία that of material cause, referring to the divine nature, and that of relational or functional cause within the Trinity. Pace Norris and Beeley, who seem to suggest that the Theologian held only one view of αἰτία, namely, a relational-efficient one,[19] the Theologian had a complex and internally coherent grasp of material and relational or functional cause within the Trinity. The key to interpreting the Trinitarian theology of Gregory's orations is to do so with an eye on semantic context: the literary units in which Gregory's references to αἰτία are found will enable the student to decide the intended meaning.

A related inquiry that may be pursued concerns the issue of whether conceiving of the divine persons in terms of substance really takes away from the relational element of God on the assumption that an immutable substance is not quite capable of responding to the situational and time-bound nature of human suffering since to do so would supposedly involve change.[20] There is, however, no logical connection between immutability of substance and inability to relate. Undergirding the presupposition that it is impossible for an unchangeable being to understand pain seems to be a libertarian view of freedom in which any course of action may possibly be taken by moral human agents, leaving the future completely unpredictable, even by God. As such, if God is to sympathize with afflicted human persons, he must of necessity grow in knowledge, of the new state of affairs, in order to respond accordingly.

Conceptually, the notion of divine immutability coheres better with an Edwardian understanding whereby freedom is defined in terms of the ability to act in accordance to one's desire, in a way that is not incompatible with a deterministic outlook on divine sovereignty.[21] As a matter of fact, Jonathan Edwards was preceded by Gregory Nyssen.[22]

---

[19] F. W. Norris, *Faith Gives Fullness to Reasoning: The Five Theological Orations of Gregory Nazianzen*, VCSup 13 (Leiden, Netherlands: E. J. Brill, 1991), pp. 135–37, 198–99, 212–13; C. A. Beeley, 'Divine Causality and the Monarchy of God the Father in Gregory of Nazianzus', *HTR* 100 (2007), pp. 200–1; *ATLA Religion Database with ATLASerials*, EBSCO*host* (accessed February 28, 2015).

[20] This seems to be the major, unchallenged presupposition in Alston's discussion of contemporary objections to substance-oriented theories of the Trinity, in 'Substance and Trinity', pp. 193–201.

[21] B. A. Ware, 'A Modified Calvinist Doctrine of God', in *Perspectives on the Doctrine of God: 4 Views*, ed. B. A. Ware (Nashville, TN: B&H Academic, 2008), pp. 99–100.

Taking this approach, it is possible to conceive of God as having always known all that is in the past, present, as well as future.

Insofar as he already knows everything in history, he was never ignorant of any matter or change in circumstances such that he has to genuinely learn of them when they actually occur in time. That being the case, from the beginning God has already determined his response to each of those incidents. History is no more than a working out in time of the eternally predetermined purposes of an unchanging God, who never grows in knowledge nor comes to be placed in a situation where he has to consider his response. In this way, divine immutability does not contradict the idea of a relationship between God and his creatures.

The absolute rule of God undermines neither the authenticity of his response to human problems nor human responsibility. Whereas the sorrow human persons experience because of one another's failings tends to be grounded in a facile comprehension of human nature in which one had a false impression of the morality of another which on exposure served to disillusion, God has a true understanding of the human person. His sorrow and anger and even hatred, therefore, do not stem from disenchantment with his human creatures so much as it arises from the abhorrence of the goodness of his being toward the godless rebelliousness that underlies myriad sinful actions that constitute its expression. Since God's response to human situations is not a function of circumstances, it is fully consistent with a view of his complete sovereignty.

Likewise, there is no conflict between the categorical sovereignty of God and the responsibility of human persons or their culpability for their sinful actions. The belief that blame cannot be assigned in a situation whereby the perpetrator could not have done otherwise is rooted in a choice-oriented perspective of culpability. According to this philosophy, a wrongdoer is to be punished because they had it in their ability to restrain themselves from doing violence but nevertheless chose to carry it out. These persons are penalized more for their foolishness, in choosing evil rather than good when they were equally capable of making the latter choice, than any inherent flaw in character.

Not to suggest that human choices are unimportant to the discussion, it is submitted that the Scripture upholds a view of God in which he abominates sin not simply because it represents a foolish choice, but fundamentally because sin in itself is abhorrent to his being.[23] More than a single, isolated outward act of disobedience against God, sin

---

[22] See L. Turcescu, 'Person', in *The Brill Dictionary of Gregory of Nyssa*, ed. L. F. Mateo-Seco and G. Maspero, trans. S. Cherney, VCSup 99 (Boston: Brill, 2010), pp. 595–6.

[23] Would Scripture otherwise use the language of wrath (Rom. 1:18–32)?

is an internal disposition of the soul that rejects the rule of God and makes pretensions to the divine glory. Those who sin are free and culpable, in that they are acting according to their desire and will, and yet captive, in that they cannot do otherwise, but nonetheless judged, because they as sinners are in and of themselves the objects of divine hatred. Consequently, the absolute sovereignty of God does not oppose the genuineness of his response to human issues or the concept of human responsibility.

The preceding discussion concerning the simplicity of God entails that God be thought of as necessarily having the specific form of being he has because it is fundamental to who he is. This raises the important question of whether in light of that God can be said to be truly free.[24] In reply, it might be underscored that classical doctrine upholds the view of God as necessarily perfect. The axiomatic implication of the claim of the necessary perfection of God is that God as he exists is incapable of imperfection. If this be so, God must be conceived, yes, as lacking freedom in the specific sense of becoming imperfect; that is, becoming anything less or other than God, since the idea of God is synonymous with that of perfection.

Contrasting his view with that of modern theologians, Beeley notes, at no point does Gregory Nazianzen perceive an irresolvable tension between his doctrine of the Father as cause and the idea of the ontological equality of the three divine persons.[25] Indeed, the concept of the relational causality of the Father, like his name, expresses and embodies the identity of substance with him of the Son and Holy Spirit. An analogue can be found in how the idea of a human son conjures up the image of another being, yet of the same nature.[26]

It is one thing to assert that the causality of the Father is compossible with and even crucial to the identity of his essence with that of the Son and the Holy Spirit, but quite another to conclude, as Christopher Beeley does, that in Gregory's thought, the three divine persons are one on account of their relationship.[27] Whether this is truly the case will be determined by the end of this survey.

Towards the end of his final theological oration, Gregory Nazianzen concludes, reiterating an earlier point by loosely quoting from the putative creedal exposition of

---

[24] One noted in McCall, 'Trinity Doctrine', pp. 53–54.

[25] C. A. Beeley, *Gregory of Nazianzus on the Trinity and the Knowledge of God: In Your Light We Shall See Light*, OSHT (Oxford: Oxford University Press, 2007), pp. 209–11.

[26] See Athanasius of Alexandria, *C. Ar.* 2.34 (Newman and Robertson, *NPNF*² 4:366).

[27] Beeley, *Gregory of Nazianzus*, p. 211.

Gregory the Wonderworker, that the oneness of God is to be found in the identical nature and purpose of the divine persons.[28]

Gregory of Nazianzus appears to be quoting from the creed of Gregory Thaumaturgus, from the conclusion, supposedly authored by him.[29] In contradistinction to his source, which uses the Greek word for Trinity, τριάς,[30] again, Gregory Nazianzen employs ἰδιότης, which refers to the divine persons. It may be asked whether this serves as evidence that the concept of monarchy, of three perfectly united co-rulers, is so central to Gregory of Nazianzus' understanding of the Trinity that he automatically reads that meaning into the word and to him monarchy is synonymous with Trinity.

If it be the case that the idea of monarchy is fundamental to Gregory's grasp of the triune nature of God, the reason that his theology of the Trinity is fit not into a framework whereby the concept of being is construed as referring to divine monarchy or 'kingliness' but one in which the concept is interpreted as pointing to 'God-ness', to the identical substance or makeup or nature, purpose, will and action of the divine persons, remains to be proffered.

The explanation is that as essential as the concept of rule is to Gregory's scheme, his starting point and indeed his goal is not a divine monarchy, with the divine persons collectively considered, but the identical nature, orientation, and action of the divine persons. This can be seen in the way he emphasizes the triple personhood of God by describing the divine substance, in itself indivisible, as present and residing in 'divided' persons.[31]

Since Gregory depicts the divine substance as capable of existing both collectively and individually, he cannot be signifying by substance a divine monarchy, because a monarchy cannot be split into parts or made to be located in an individual, but encompasses the three divine persons and, as a matter of fact, the universe they administer. Nor could the being of God be expressed in terms of a perfect capacity to govern, for the same cause: the divine substance in the view of Gregory exists both individually and collectively. If the meaning of the concept of divine being were restricted to the sense of ability, it would not be able to fully encompass the collective phenomenon of the monarchy, which involves more than ability.

---

[28] Gregory of Nazianzus, *Or.* 31.28.

[29] A translation of the creed is furnished by J. T. Law, *A Catechetical Exposition of the Apostles' Creed* (London: C. and J. Rivington, 1825), p. 28.

[30] Gregory Thaumaturgus, *Exp. fid.* (PG 10:1a); 'τριάς', *LSJ* 2:1816.

[31] Gregory of Nazianzus, *Or.* 31.14.

In light of the foregoing, it is more logical and coherent to read Gregory as saying that the divine substance has to do with the makeup, orientation, and action of the divine persons rather than divine monarchy or kingliness. The former exist both in the divine persons considered individually and collectively and, with the persons, constitute the divine monarchy.

Oratio 39

Christopher Beeley has claimed that because the Theological Orations cannot really be isolated from their polemical context, those who would discover Gregory of Nazianzus' position on the Trinity must look in his other orations. Weighing in on the issue, Verna Harrison has highlighted Gregory's festal orations as significant.[32] One of these is the thirty-ninth oration on the baptism of Christ, which she has translated. Two paragraphs in particular from this oration are worth careful examination.[33]

Prescinding from the previous discussion of the Theological Orations, and working out anew Gregory's concept of the divine being beginning with this oration, it may be observed that the Theologian identifies the one that is in God with words denoting the divine nature. This in itself, along with the reference to the divine nature being within the three persons, suffices as an explicit statement of the concept of the being of God as substance as possessed by the divine persons. Consequently, Gregory Nazianzen espouses a doctrine of the divine being as the substance that, being one, subsists in equal degree and without increase or diminution in the three divine persons.

Yet, as if in order that no doubt should be cast on his doctrine, Gregory affirms and further develops his understanding of the divine being in the following paragraph.[34] Gregory the Theologian uses the scriptural testimony to the inseparability of divine operation to assert the identical nature of the three divine persons,[35] an argument found also in Gregory Nyssen.

---

[32] V. E. F. Harrison, 'Illumined From All Sides By The Trinity: Neglected Themes in Gregory's Trinitarian Theology', in *Re-Reading Gregory of Nazianzus: Essays on History, Theology, and Culture*, ed. C. A. Beeley, CUA Studies in Early Christianity (Washington, D.C.: The Catholic University of America Press, 2012), pp. 14-15.

[33] Gregory of Nazianzus, *Or.* 39.11 (Harrison, PPS).

[34] Gregory of Nazianzus, *Or.* 39.12 (Harrison, PPS).

[35] An observation of Ayres and Barnes, as noted by Harrison, 'Illumined From All Sides By The Trinity', p. 13.

More than that, the Father, Son, and Holy Spirit are described as working in different dimensions of the same activity or action within the created sphere, and consequently demonstrated to be cognitive and conative entities capable of performing the single act of creation; cognitive because the act of creation requires rationality, and a supreme one at that, and conative because, in Gregory's scheme of the divine being, the being of God is substance, and so there is nothing above and beyond the divine person to motivate them to engage in the work of creation, which can only be accounted for by will, which, in turn, makes for self[36] and therefore consciousness, even a center of consciousness.

This is in light of the fact that the divine person has a concept of self, making him a subject—seeing that introspection signifies an objectification of self by self, which functions as subject, thereby establishing the subjectivity of the one engaged in introspection—which possesses cognitive and conative capacities, as well as an awareness of the environment.[37]

Furthermore, the divine substance subsists to an equal degree and in its fullness in each divine person. For this reason, the motivation and desire must arise from the persons of the Father, Son, and Holy Spirit themselves, and exist equally and fully in each of them; as such, these divine persons also possess selves and consciousness. Harrison

---

[36] The exercise of the faculty of will or volition presupposes the involvement of a subject, without which it is impossible; a statement like 'I want to eat' is not complete in the absence of a subject.

[37] This is in concord with the interpretations of Paul Fedwick and Lucian Turcescu concerning Gregory of Nyssa's concept of divine personhood. Fedwick, in the foreword to *Gregory of Nyssa and the Concept of Divine Persons* by L. Turcescu, AAR Academy Series (Oxford: Oxford University Press, 2005), p. x, underscores in Gregory's understanding of divine personhood the elements of selfhood and will. Turcescu in *Gregory of Nyssa and the Concept of Divine Persons*, AAR Academy Series (Oxford: Oxford University Press, 2005), p. 5 disavows the idea of a complete equivalence with a modern idea of personhood and yet avers that in Nyssen's theology, there is an understanding of the divine person which incorporates ideas of a self (the divine person wants something for himself; namely, to conform to good and be what he is, implying that he is conscious of his self, and as a subject with assertive capacity has a concept of self); a will; and an awareness of the environment (this implied by the fact that he is able to choose virtue, suggesting ability to make a moral choice and presupposing a capacity for interaction with the environment). Consequently, although Turcescu is opposed to reading a modern notion of personhood as a center of consciousness from Gregory Nyssen's discussions of divine personhood, he would arguably not disagree with the notion of a divine person as a center of consciousness understood, as is the case throughout this study, as an entity that possesses self-awareness, cognition, conation, and environmental awareness.

adduces Gregory Nazianzen's ethical extrapolations from his doctrine of the immanent Trinity in support of a 'psychological' view of the divine persons.[38]

Oratio 40

Gregory of Nazianzus offers a vision of the immanent Trinity from a human perspective in his fortieth oration, also a festal one.[39] Evidently, the Theologian is thinking of the idea of 'God' in two different senses when he speaks of the persons as being individually and collectively God. A first signification is of God as the title given to each divine person by virtue of his possession of the divine nature. The second sense is of God as the single, unified rule of the Trinity, the 'monarchy' and action of the three divine persons in rule over the created order.

Concerning Gregory's comments about the inseparability of the three and one, they are to be understood as being made from a human perspective of the Trinity. A divine person cannot be contemplated in isolation from the other two, since they are always together, in one another. Moreover, since each person is infinite in glory, it is impossible to fully take in even one divine person, and to move from that one to another. Yet if one thinks of the three divine persons from a broader angle, all that one sees is a single light, because they exist, live, and act in complete unity, oneness, and togetherness. As if to silence every peradventure concerning his position on the divine being, Gregory Nazianzen simply declares in his forty-second oration that the qualitatively identical nature of the divine persons is God.[40]

---

[38] Harrison, 'Illumined From All Sides By The Trinity', pp. 22–26.

[39] Gregory of Nazianzus, *Or.* 40.41 (Harrison, PPS).

[40] Gregory of Nazianzus, *Or.* 42.15 (Browne and Swallow, *NPNF*² 7:390). Meyendorff renders the final clause in a similar way. J. Meyendorff, *Byzantine Theology: Historical Trends and Doctrinal Themes*, 2nd ed. (New York: Fordham University Press, 1983), p. 183. The Greek reads: Φύσις δὲ τοῖς τρισὶ μία, Θεός. Gregory of Nazianzus, *Or.* 42 (PG 36:15b).

Chapter 4

Gregory of Nyssa

De Sancta Trinitate

Like the other two Cappadocian Fathers, the writings ascribed, truly or falsely, to Gregory Nyssen, brother of Basil of Caesarea, convey a conception of the divine being in terms of qualities, purpose, and actions rather than specific personal reality.[1] In his[2] treatise to Eustathius on the Trinity, repeatedly Gregory of Nyssa refers to the godhead or divine being as an attribute, signifying the ability to rule the created order, and the nature and particular shape of that rule. As a case in point, this occurs as he sets forth the position of those who deny the deity of the Holy Spirit while affirming that of the Father and the Son.[3]

---

[1] One of these points has been noted by Erickson in writing about Gregory Nyssen's theology of the Trinity in *God in Three Persons: A Contemporary Interpretation of the Trinity* (Grand Rapids, Mich.: Baker Books, 1995), p. 93. Stephen Holmes observes that in Gregory's view, the divine being exists in three entities with the same will and action in *The Quest for the Trinity: The Doctrine of God in Scripture, History and Modernity* (Downers Grove, IL: IVP Academic, 2012), p. 109. See also D. Brown, *The Divine Trinity* (La Salle, IL: Open Court, 1985), p. 294.

[2] The treatise is attributed by some to Basil of Caesarea, among whose letters it is found, in a truncated form as *Ep.* 189 (in the Benedictine arrangement). H. A. Wilson, 'His Teaching on the Holy Trinity', in *Nicene and Post-Nicene Fathers*, Second Series 5 (New York: Cosimo Classics, 2007), p. 25. Again, for purposes of convenience, the ascription to Gregory is accepted.

[3] Gregory of Nyssa, *Sanct. Trin.* GNO 3.1:7.9–11 (Wilson, *NPNF*² 5:327); the word translated with the meaning of property of being is ὄνομα, signifying name in the sense of title, which evokes the notion of an attribute or character of nature for which it is given.

The thrust of his thesis that the Holy Spirit is to be accorded recognition as divine is primarily based on the tacit assumption that there is a single indivisible unique divine substance or makeup described by a variety of qualities such as beneficence, purity, non-temporality, sagacity, morality, preeminence, and power.[4] This presupposition, coupled with the scriptural observation that the Holy Spirit possesses all the qualities possessed by the Father and the Son, leads naturally to the conclusion that the Holy Spirit shares with them in the attribute of divinity if He shares in the aforementioned qualities because His possession of the qualities of the Father and Son indicates a sharing in the same divine substance.[5]

One point which deserves clarification concerns the use of adjectives expressing attribute paired with a personal relative pronoun as though a specific personal reality was in view rather than a conception of the divine being in terms of qualities, purpose and actions.

It is worth noting that, in the first case, adjectives of attribute may be applied even to impersonal things, as in the instances of 'good conduct', 'wise decision', 'mighty deed', 'righteous action'. In the second case, the objection can be addressed by recourse to doctrinal consistency; if Gregory Nyssen were indeed in the part highlighted referring not to divine substance but to one particular divine person, he would have to speak of three subjects instead of 'one subject', given that the attributes apply equally to the Father and the Son and the Holy Spirit, so that the relative pronoun is better rendered impersonally rather than personally.

It is more likely, however, and in keeping with the translation of the relative pronoun as personal, to suppose that Gregory has in mind not the random throwing out of an epithet by someone without specifically intending a signification pointing to either Father, Son or Holy Spirit, but that in speaking or writing of, say, the one who is beneficent or sagacious, the speaker or writer was thinking of one of the three divine persons, and he could have been thinking of any one of the three persons, considering that no divine person has a monopoly, as it were, of any of the attributes.[6]

A little later, Gregory Nyssen introduces a qualification: usage of the name of divinity does not encompass all that the divine nature signifies, as if human beings could con-

---

[4] Gregory of Nyssa, *Sanct. Trin.* GNO 3.1:7.25–26 (Wilson, *NPNF*² 5:327).

[5] Gregory of Nyssa, *Sanct. Trin.* GNO 3.1:7.17–9.8 (Wilson, *NPNF*² 5:327–28).

[6] This is such that even if the author were, in the course of the discussion, to abruptly employ a different epithet than that with which he began, such as changing from 'the Wise' to 'the Mighty', the hearer or reader could still have the confidence that no change in subject was being intended.

template the divine essence in a more direct fashion as they do, say, natural objects, and thereby compress their far greater understanding of their essence into a term of reference. The truth is that human beings know not what they utter when they speak of a divine essence, except that which the operations of the divine nature reveals to them in the revelation that the divine persons have allowed. Be that as it may, it remains important to be able to predicate something of the divine persons if human beings are indeed to discourse about them in a meaningful way.

Gregory appears to be attempting to avoid the error of those who claim that everything about the divine nature may be comprehended and that the name of divinity embraces the full signification of the divine nature, when he disputes the identification of the name of divinity with the divine nature.

In Anatolios' helpful discussion of Gregory Nyssen's idea of the human inability to know the divine nature, Nyssen defines knowledge of essence as a complete and exhaustive understanding of the mind of a being that enables prediction of its every act or response and an absolute knowledge of its origin.[7] The writer believes it is fair to say that no one completely knows the mind of God because God has revealed it to no one to that degree but also because the full comprehension of that infinite mind far exceeds the finite capacity of the human mind, to say nothing of how it is impossible to grasp the origin of God, for there is none in the first instance.

More can be said about Gregory's claim that the name of divinity signifies divine operation rather than divine nature. This is by no means an assertion pertaining to qualitative difference between the two but rather an immeasurable quantitative distinction. There is a definite difference between the signification of any term used to speak about the divine being, and that being itself. To employ an example, when the divine being is spoken of in Scripture as 'good', this may be done on the basis of a divine act that rescued Israel from her Egyptian oppressors and brought her into the land of promise. The Christian reader may add to the concept of deliverance the redemptive work of the Lord Jesus. Yet, do these time and space-bound events adequately communicate the essence or meaning of God? One must disagree.

Human categories, which express what is finite since humans can only express what they have experienced and no human experience is infinite so that the experiences they express are by nature finite, can never encapsulate that which is infinite so that even if

---

[7] K. Anatolios, *Retrieving Nicaea: The Development and Meaning of Trinitarian Doctrine* (Grand Rapids, MI: Baker Academic, 2011), pp. 160–63.

goodness were the defining quality of God,[8] the meaning signified would still be inadequate to convey the essence of God. Above all, words are simply pointers to things which have been perceived; the divine essence being beyond human perception, and therefore forever removed from human experience, is not and cannot ever be communicated by any word or set of words. As a result, in a significant sense, the term 'God' or even 'divine nature' cannot be said to signify just that—the divine nature.

To take an analogy, necessarily inadequate, the divine being could be likened to the Pacific Ocean in a world in which it is impossible to gain access to or even conceive that body of water or for that matter any body of water. In this alternate reality, completely devoid of water, the object that most closely approximates the Pacific Ocean is a single drop of water, kept in an air-tight container. Suppose that this drop of water represents the human conception of the divine being. It would be absurd at best to claim that the drop of water *is* the Pacific Ocean. Similarly, it is ludicrous to assert that 'God' or the 'divine being', as used and understood by finite human beings, actually refers to the reality to which it points. What it really denotes is the finite human understanding of God, the drop of water, and not the Pacific Ocean, the essence of God. In this respect, Nyssen does not err in pronouncing on the categorical inadequacy of human conceptions to communicate the divine essence in any way.

Nonetheless, one might differentiate between the concept of the divine essence as bearer of meaning and as reference. As signifier, the human conception fails spectacularly at conveying the meaning of the divine essence. Yet, as reference, it serves as a signpost indicating the infinite without signifying it. Terms conventionally used of God may continue to be fruitfully applied, but always with the fittingly humble acknowledgement that in so doing one is pointing to the essence without actually speaking about it. A man as personally acquainted with God as Moses[9] can no more claim to have acquired accurate knowledge of the divine essence than anyone can in feeling a drop of water claim to know exactly what the Pacific Ocean is like.

In a sense, human comprehension of God via divine revelation differs from the truth of the divine essence only in degree, given that God has already qualitatively definitively disclosed himself to people through the Son. Yet, this quantitative difference is an innumerable one. Even in the human realm, some precision is attached to use of the word '(to) know'. Not everyone can be said to have real knowledge of any subject matter.

---

[8] As for Basil, according to Andrew Radde-Gallwitz in *Basil of Caesarea, Gregory of Nyssa, and the Transformation of Divine Simplicity*, OECS (Oxford: Oxford University Press, 2009), p. 173.

[9] Or any other exemplary biblical character for that matter.

Among those who have been exposed to content on the topic, a distinction can be struck between those who 'know' the subject and those who do not. Reading a few lines from a book on economics does not make one a person knowledgeable in the discipline. At the same time, one is not required to have read every single book on a subject and synthesized their content in order to be said to know the subject. By implication, there is a particular point at which one crosses from the realm of non-knowledge to that of knowledge.

At what point can one be said to know the divine essence? Perchance another analogy might be in order. If the divine essence were an unending ladder to heaven, in a world where heaven is a physical location, although one situated an infinite distance away, could a man who had seen as much of the ladder as his eyes allowed him truthfully boast that he has seen the heavenly ladder? Such a claim would not be factually accurate, for he did not actually see the entire ladder.

He may know how the rest of the ladder looks, and perhaps fool himself into thinking his imagination has captured the entire structure or approximated it to some degree, but the fact remains that he has not really seen the ladder. Due to his inherent limitation of sight, there is no possibility of taking in the whole structure. At most, he could lay claim to having espied an *infinitely small* part of the ladder to heaven.[10] Similarly, some may believe they have attained knowledge of the divine essence through human ideas and even the record of the life of the incarnate Son of God.[11]

Still, no sensible person can lay claim to having actually seen the divine essence. The things people know they know by direct experience or analogues that facilitate knowledge. Experience is the basis of meaning and of knowledge. To be sure, it is fully possible to contrive ideas of things that do not actually exist. Yet no imagination is entirely original and distinct from reality. Every theme that human beings have explored has been that which is amenable to their finite comprehension. For all the centuries of contemplation, people have come no closer to an understanding of the infinite divine essence, including Christians, who have but seen the foot of the heavenly ladder. They have neither seen the divine essence, nor can they conceive it. In this respect, then, it may and must be confidently affirmed that human beings have no knowledge of the divine essence, though Christians do have some very important and qualitatively definitive knowledge of God. Just as the person in the illustration of the ladder to heaven can only

---

[10] To use a paradoxical expression.
[11] Mullins, 'An Analytic Response', pp. 90–91.

say that he has seen an *infinitely small* part of it, so Christians can say that they have come to know an *infinitely small* part of God.[12]

In this manner, in disputing the identification of the name of divinity with the nature of God, Nyssen is not, as it may be supposed, contradicting what he has only lately established about what can be known about God, also considering that he goes on to elucidate how he as a theologian arrives at the conclusion that the natures of the Father, Son and Holy Spirit are one by means of the observation that their operations are identical, as in the processes of sanctification, in which the Lord asserts the Father in John 17:11 and 17:17, as well as the Holy Spirit, is an actor, and of the revelation of the divine nature to creatures.[13]

Ad Ablabium

If Gregory of Nyssa concludes that the natures of the divine persons are one by means of their indivisibility of united action, he is not redefining the concept of divine being as divine action, as Jenson supposes.[14] Even in one of the two texts on which he bases his assertion, Gregory's letter to Ablabius, he affirms that understanding of the divine nature is possible to the degree to which the divine persons reveal themselves through their operation; and that that means of revelation of the divine nature, while revealing

---

[12] This clarification is inspired by Gregory Nyssen's stricture in *Ad Graecos* concerning how one may properly speak not of three human beings but only of three hypostases or instantiations of the human being. Tangentially related to the present discussion, in view of the use of the concepts of the qualities of being 'unending' and 'infinite', it is to be noted that the bridge of which it is said that it is unending, is really not as such, but rather 'infinite'. That which is unending is of necessity not infinite, and that which is infinite is of necessity not simply unending. By definition, that which does not end can be measured, since it only makes sense to say of something which is limited and quantifiable that it never does end; if something were already infinite, how might it be increased? Therefore, it can be said of time, and God's human creatures, that they are of unending duration and lifespan; but only of God that he has infinite life. From the timeless divine perspective, and in divine eternity, human creatures, and time itself, being unending yet not infinite, do not have any real existence, but subsist simply as thoughts in the divine being.

[13] Gregory of Nyssa, *Sanct. Trin.* GNO 3.1:10.14–13.21 (Wilson, *NPNF*² 5:328-29).

[14] R. W. Jenson, *The Triune Identity: God According to the Gospel* (Philadelphia, PA: Fortress Press, 1982), p. 113.

something of that divine nature at the same time that it (the divine operation) fully reveals its own nature, does not fully reveal that divine nature.[15]

He illustrates his point by recourse to the way in which the Greek term for the godhead, θεότης, a cognate of θέα, meaning beholding, originated from the observation that God sees and knows all, even the thoughts of people and things invisible.[16] As can be seen, Gregory does not change the meaning of 'God' to operations of the same, in which case he would have said that θεός signifies not the beholder but the act of beholding.

Drawing his essay to a close, Gregory furnishes a more lucid understanding of the divine nature when he refers to it in terms of sovereignty and activity, finding an analogy in the divine appointment of Moses as deity to Pharaoh (Exod. 7:1), showing that he conceives of the divine being as providential, sovereign and completely harmonious rule.[17]

As such, to speak of the Father, Son and Holy Spirit as divine, is to speak of them as having precisely the same makeup and purpose and engaging in the very same actions as co-sovereigns of the universe, presiding over and directing the affairs of the world with the same mind, will, and purpose, and in exactly the same manner, with no dissension or division whatsoever but only the most sublime and perfect harmony.

Gregory's treatise addressed to a certain Ablabius removes any doubt there may be that he holds an impersonal view of the divine substance. In that work, he essays to expound the reason that the fathers of the church do not refer to three divine persons as three Gods though it is common to designate three human persons collectively as three men.

Prior to enunciating his understanding, Gregory turns his attention to proving the inadequacy of language in communicating the concept of the divine being. This is because terms employed to describe the divine substance do so by way of a negative signification, expressing something by saying what it is not rather than saying what it is, an instance being a word that signifies an incapacity to suffer corruption, or in terms of an action, like a title that refers to a purveyor of vitality, leaving unexplained the substance of the doer of the deed; even if a word could correctly express an aspect of the divine

---

[15] Gregory of Nyssa, *Abl.* PG 45:121a (Wilson, *NPNF*² 5:332). It should be noted that references to the Greek text of Gregory's letter to Ablabius indicate the page number in the PG in lieu of the usual section number because the text is not divided into sections.

[16] Gregory of Nyssa, *Abl.* PG 45:121d (Wilson, *NPNF*² 5:333).

[17] Gregory of Nyssa, *Sanct. Trin.* GNO 3.1:14.5–7 (Wilson, *NPNF*² 5:329).

nature, in the final analysis, as Gregory would later assert, there is no way a word, which is by nature finite, could come close to fully expressing the infinite and ineffable substance of the divine.[18]

His exposition of linguistic inadequacy in capturing the meaning of the concept of the divine being is by no means digressive, but the lynchpin of his theory concerning the impropriety of speaking of the three divine persons as multiple Gods. If the divine persons can only be described in terms of the revelation of their activity to humankind, and if the activity or operation of the divine persons is one, each responsible for a dimension of the same activity which all undertake alike, the Father being responsible for the idea, the Son for the decision, and the Holy Spirit, the execution, it is only possible to speak in terms of one divine actor though one may refer to three subjects of one divine action. He contrasts the divine persons with human persons, who while engaged in the same profession do not altogether produce one action out of their efforts so that it is justified to speak of them in the plural.[19]

The three divine persons perform the same action in a non-composite way; that is, they do not perform a collective action that is made up of individual 'actions' that each performs, but they are each responsible for a different dimension of the same action.[20] Each performs his own respective role in perfect coordination and harmony with the rest, presupposing an individual consciousness, rationality, will, and ability in each divine person, the prerequisites for a cognitive and conative agent, a reinforcement of an earlier argument in favor of the divine persons as three cognitive and conative centers of consciousness in the thought of the Cappadocians.[21] These arguments exclude the possibility of contending that the divine persons might be non-sentient agents pre-programmed as it were with the instructions to carry out the same functions.

Aside from those logical conclusions, Gregory Nyssen demonstrates in the passage most recently cited that he is not thinking of the persons as abstractions or phases in a process of action, or as automatons. On the contrary, he recognizes that his conception of the divine persons, apart from accurate understanding, is vulnerable to the perception that he is presenting the Father, Son, and Holy Spirit as three Gods. His attempt to prevent the misconception of tritheism consists simply in his redefinition of the divine be-

---

[18] Gregory of Nyssa, *Abl.* PG 45:121b–c (Wilson, *NPNF*² 5:332–33); idem., *Abl.* PG 45:129c (Wilson, *NPNF*² 5:335).

[19] Gregory of Nyssa, *Abl.* PG 45:125c–d, 127a–c (Wilson, *NPNF*² 5:334).

[20] J. D. Zizioulas, *Lectures in Christian Dogmatics* (London: T&T Clark, 2008), pp. 72.

[21] See the section on Basil of Caesarea.

ing in terms of the singularity of divine action: God, properly speaking, does not signify a concrete entity of divine nature so that to speak of the Father, Son, and Holy Spirit is to speak of three Gods; instead, God properly designates the common and qualitatively identical nature of the three divine persons expressed in their complete unity of action. It is a oneness of substance and action that is in view, a qualitative identity and oneness of essence rather than a quantitative oneness of the essence of the divine persons, as Holmes avers.[22]

Richard Cross rightly expresses by way of theological implication at the end of his study of Gregory's doctrine of universals that the divine being fundamentally signifies nature.[23] If 'God' denotes the divine substance that exists in the three divine persons, to maintain that these persons are insentient is tantamount to turning the reality of God, as instantiated in the Father, the Son, and the Holy Spirit, into something even less than a human being.

On two counts, consequently, those of Gregory's doctrines of inseparable divine operations, and of the divine being, Gregory shows that he is manifestly not teaching a doctrine of insentient divine persons, but one where the same are socio-psychological entities. If this were not the truth, Gregory would not suspect that his theology might be misinterpreted as upholding a view of three Gods. Moreover, if Nyssen was indeed of the view that the divine persons are insentient factors which bear little resemblance to human persons, he would have made that clear, particularly given the fact that in the letter in question he was dealing with an analogy which compares the divine and human persons. Gregory's silence in the form of his lack of objection here may be said to speak volumes about his specific profession concerning divine personhood.

For the above reasons, it appears prima facie that the claim by Sarah Coakley to the effect that in the writing of Gregory of Nyssa, in particular, his letter to Ablabius, the divine persons do not necessarily possess individuated consciousness[24] must be rejected as spurious. Yet the complexity of Coakley's argument means that a more nuanced response is required, for she intimates by her juxtaposition of ideas of individuated consciousness and autonomy and the contrast she draws between those and a concept of the divine persons as expressing a perfect harmony of wills[25] that she is not simply op-

---

[22] Holmes, *Quest for the Trinity*, p. 108.

[23] Cross, 'Gregory of Nyssa', p. 408.

[24] S. Coakley, "'Persons' in the 'Social' Doctrine of the Trinity: A Critique of Current Analytic Discussion', in *The Trinity: An Interdisciplinary Symposium on the Trinity*, ed. S. T. Davis, D. Kendall, and G. O'Collins (Oxford: Oxford University Press, 2002), p. 133.

[25] Ibid., p. 137.

posing the idea of *distinct* socio-psychological centers for each divine person but one of distinct socio-psychological centers with actually or possibly *differing* wills for each divine person.

Accordingly, there are at least three ways of understanding divine personhood: one, the divine persons are characterized by a single socio-psychological center; two, the divine persons are characterized by distinct socio-psychological centers but being of the same substance possess the same will; three, the divine persons are characterized by distinct socio-psychological centers and being of different substances possess different wills. Be that as it may, Coakley does not seem to acknowledge the second possibility in that she seemly writes of the divine persons that they are to be distinguished solely by their different locations or roles in the same divine action.[26]

Whilst it is imperative to agree with Coakley that the divine persons may not be posited as having different wills, this need not preclude a conception of the persons as having distinct socio-psychological centers. In this way, to the degree that Coakley refutes the notion of *differing* wills among the divine persons, she takes a perspective with which the writer of this study is in agreement; but to the degree that she is against the idea of *distinct* yet qualitatively though not numerically identical wills among the divine persons, she departs from the view of the writer.

John Behr draws a similar conclusion to the one given in this study about the respective roles of the divine persons highlighted previously with the Father conceptualizing, the Son executing, and the Holy Spirit completing the action of God.[27] If it is asked how the divine persons might be associated with distinctive dimensions of activities in which the three are inseparably and singly engaged, and yet have primary responsibility for certain actions, like the incarnation in the case of the Son, it may perhaps be highlighted that these peculiar core activities with which a certain divine person is connected are intimately related with the dimension of divine operation under his purview. Therefore, in regard to the act of becoming human, this is the Son's in a special way because it is an act that more than anything else 'activates' or 'brings into effect', in particular, the kingdom of God.

The concept of respective divine roles, entered into by choice, constitutes an important way to understand the hierarchical relations between the divine persons. Hierar-

---

[26] Ibid., pp. 132, 137. Citation a part of Gregory of Nyssa, *Abl.* PG 45:125c–d, 127a–c (Wilson, *NPNF*² 5:334); see discussion above.

[27] J. Behr, *The Nicene Faith*, vol. 2 of *The Formation of Christian Theology* (Crestwood, NY: St. Vladimir's Seminary Press, 2004), 2:431.

chy in the relations between the divine persons is the picture afforded by Scripture, as Thomas Smail has observed.[28]

It is legitimately asked, as Gruenler has in the course of his argument against differential relations between the Father, Son and Holy Spirit, whether hierarchical divine relations are descriptive of the Trinity solely in economic rather than also in immanent terms. If divine hierarchy is a factor only in the economic Trinity, it would be hard to comprehend the significance of the divine names of Father and Son, words which carry an inherent sense of functional inequality.[29]

To return to the previous train of thought, ontologically equal divine persons have always been committed, in accordance with the unchangeable divine plan, to the respective roles of the Father, Son, and Holy Spirit, so that the one in the functionally superior role attains and voluntarily accepts that functional superiority by the voluntary submission of his functional subordinates, a superiority which he does not possess in himself ontologically.

Robert Letham notes that patristic defenders of orthodoxy employed the idea of an order or τάξις to denote an arrangement that is fitting in that the roles of the Father, Son, and Holy Spirit are fitting and perfect ones.[30] It is needful to ground the divine hierarchy in terms of role and not nature not merely to obviate the problem of contradicting the doctrine of the ontological equality possessed by the divine persons but also to avert the need to account for the non-transference of the distinctive qualities of each person, be it the unbegottenness of the Father, or the begottenness of the Son, or the processional nature of the Holy Spirit, to the other persons.

This is no less than an assertion that what is unique to each divine person, apart from his individual consciousness, is not inherent to the person, but the result of a commitment to their respective central roles that has always existed as per the divine plan, so that there was never a time when the Father, Son or Holy Spirit were not who they now are, and there is no possibility of a switching of roles. Such a scheme meets the condition for the divine hierarchy in which the roles do not indicate ontological superi-

---

[28] T. A. Smail, *Like Father, Like Son: The Trinity Imaged in Our Humanity* (Milton Keynes, UK: Paternoster, 2005), pp. 159–200.

[29] R. G. Gruenler, *The Trinity in the Gospel of John: A Thematic Commentary on the Fourth Gospel* (Eugene, OR: Wipf and Stock, 2004), p. xiv.

[30] R. Letham, *The Holy Trinity: In Scripture, History, Theology, and Worship* (Phillipsburg, NJ: P&R, 2004), pp. 400, 483, 491.

ority, in the case of those of the Father and the Son, or ontological inferiority, in the case of those of the Son and the Holy Spirit, highlighted by Jürgen Moltmann.[31]

In this way, the charge of Aëtius and Eunomius concerning the irrationality of affirming that the three divine persons share in one substance without also embracing the idea that the unbegottenness of the Father is shared with the Son and therefore undermining the concept of the distinctiveness of the divine persons, is taken seriously, as it must be, and addressed.[32] Thus, also, the eternal generation of the Son may be understood, in terms of an assumption of a role.[33]

The contemporary debate among evangelicals apropos of a possible subordination of the Son to the Father, to which Giles has been an active contributor, sheds light on the importance of holding in tension both the equality of the nature of the divine persons as well as the voluntary submission of the Son and the Spirit to the Father. A solution to the issue cannot be sought by arguing, as Giles seems to do, that the difference between the divine persons does not consist in some form of submission, thus emptying 'Father' and 'Son' of their functional significance, so as to safeguard the equality of the nature of the divine persons, as though role and function has to be conceptualized in terms of nature.[34] This is alien to the thought of the Cappadocians.[35]

To a certain degree, Gregory's argument from the divine operation bears a likeness to his argument from the divine nature, of which he is less in favor given his realization that no concept of language could ever approximate the comprehensive articulation of the reality of the divine substance. According to that line of thought, which begins from the assumption that human beings could comprehend the divine substance, the divine persons are spoken of as one God in spite of being three because they share one nature, and this has precedents in the concepts of organized civic or military groups of people, all of which contain plurality in terms that are used as though they were those denoting single entities. As a matter of fact, according to Gregory, properly speaking, the term

---

[31] J. Moltmann, *The Trinity and the Kingdom: The Doctrine of God*, trans. M. Kohl (Minneapolis, MN: Fortress Press, 1993), pp. 175–76.

[32] G. L. Prestige, *God in Patristic Thought* (Eugene, OR: Wipf & Stock, 2008), p. 152; Eunomius of Cyzicus, *Apol.* 1.9 (Vaggione, OECT).

[33] Prestige, *God in Patristic Thought*, p. 149.

[34] K. Giles, *Jesus and the Father: Modern Evangelicals Reinvent the Doctrine of the Trinity* (Grand Rapids, MI: Zondervan, 2006), pp. 205–41.

[35] E. J. Fortman, *The Triune God: A Historical Study of the Doctrine of the Trinity* (Grand Rapids, MI: Baker Book House, 1972), pp. 82–83.

'man' should not be used in the plural but only in the singular because 'man' denotes human nature and there is only one human nature.[36]

Gregory takes up the same point and expands on it in a later part of his essay.[37] The analogy which Gregory employs of gold coins reveals again his qualitative understanding of the meaning of the concept of the being of God, for the illustration would be applicable only if he intended to liken the divine being or substance to the substance or material of gold.

Having reviewed two pertinent passages, the time has come to examine the thrust of Gregory's argument regarding why there is no error of logical coherence in proclaiming the three divine persons as a single God, which is as follows: as already mentioned, the Nyssen concept of God has to do with a particular and peculiar substance, orientation, and action. That 'God' has a certain kind of substance as referent, rather than a number of different kinds of the same, fulfills the criterion of singleness.

For lack of scintillating creativity, this may be better grasped by comparison to the quality of being exactly 100 degrees Celsius. Suppose that the word 'hot' were attached specifically to items of that temperature and none other. Then suppose for the sake of argument that there were only three items in the world, at the point of consideration, which possessed that specific quality. Though there were three objects, we would not thereby suggest that the quality of hotness had increased in quantity, so that instead of being one, hotness had become three, entailing a reference not to a single hotness but three 'hotnesses'. Likewise, in a theology such as Gregory's which posits 'God' as a specific quality, there is ever only one kind of it, even if there may be three instances of the same.

While this perspective of Nyssen's concept of the divine being seems to do justice to the contexts of the passages analyzed, another view has been propounded, namely, that of a term significant of human essence in the first of the two most immediately cited passages as the entirety of the human race.[38] Johannes Zachhuber appears to be concerned to make sense of Gregory's perplexing analogical juxtaposition of the relationship between the single concept of the human nature and multiple human individuals to that existing between a collective human entity like an army, assembly, people, mob, and the plurality embedded in those concepts. This can be seen in the way he broaches the issue

---

[36] Gregory of Nyssa, *Abl.* PG 45:117d, 119a–b (Wilson, *NPNF*² 5:332).

[37] Gregory of Nyssa, *Abl.* PG 45:129d, 131a–c (Wilson, *NPNF*² 5:335–36).

[38] J. Zachhuber, 'Once Again: Gregory of Nyssa on Universals', *JTS* ns 56 no 1 (April 2005). *ATLA Religion Database with ATLASerials*, EBSCO*host* (accessed August 16, 2015). Citation from p. 89.

of an apparent tension between a conception of the human essence in its straightforward sense and the illustration of collective nouns.³⁹

At issue is the purpose of the analogy. Is Nyssen drawing an analogy of equation, asserting that human nature is comparable to a collective human entity? This does not seem to be the case, considering that he is comparing two relationships rather than equating the first and second subjects of two clauses, and given the fact that the contexts of the discussion of the human essence as highlighted in the foregoing dictate that the concept be interpreted in terms of substance. As such, it may at most be granted that Gregory is making an analogy of formal rather than substantial likeness: the relationship between human nature and multiple human individuals is comparable to that between a collective human entity and its individual human constituents in that both involve the idea of a single, or singly viewed, object which presupposes plurality. Accordingly, we can continue to maintain that the text articulates a concept of the divine being as substance.

Ad Graecos

The same idea is present in the Nyssen's discussion on the significance of the name of divinity: *Ad Graecos (Ex communibus notionibus)*. While Daniel Stramara has argued in the introduction to his English translation of the tractate that the work is mainly concerned with the exposition of πρόσωπον, rather than abstract terms that have to do with the one and three in the divine being, that Gregory is there seeking from the first to expound the meaning of the concept of God or the divine being can hardly be gainsaid, as the subsequent investigation will attempt to prove.⁴⁰

From the outset, Gregory of Nyssa defines his understanding of the being of God in terms of nature.⁴¹ This quintessential twofold claim that 'God' properly refers to the divine substance, and the three divine persons are each worthy of the title 'God' only in

---

³⁹ Ibid., p. 81.
⁴⁰ D. F. Stramara, Jr., 'Gregory of Nyssa, *Ad Graecos* "How It Is That We Say There Are Three Persons In The Divinity But Do Not Say There Are Three Gods"* (To The Greeks: Concerning The Commonality Of Concepts)', *GOTR* 41, no. 4 (1996), p. 377. *ATLA Religion Database with ATLASerials*, EBSCO*host* (accessed September 2, 2015). The text of the treatise is found in pp. 381–91.
⁴¹ Gregory of Nyssa, *Comm. not.* (Stramara, 381–83). The same point is reiterated in pp. 382 and 383.

virtue of their divine nature or substance or essence allows Gregory Nyssen to dismiss two objections.

The concept of the divine being as substance furnishes the means to address the assertion that the Father, Son, and Holy Spirit are of different essences since it is possible for more than one concrete thing to be of the same substance, as in the case of human beings where entities with different substances are classed under things that possess the broader category of a 'human' substance.[42]

Yet the assaults on the logic of the Trinitarian doctrine have not thereby ceased. A second challenge that confronts Gregory of Nyssa takes him to task for contending for two different senses of 'God'. As already established from the text, Nyssen is not equivocal in regard to his conception of the divine being, which he comprehends in an essential sense, and, only by extension, in a titular sense. His opponents, however, fail to grasp his ideas in their remarkable clarity and coherence and force a choice between his primary essential and secondary and derivative titular notions of 'God'. Incapable of apprehending a two-level understanding of the name of divinity, they subject their misinterpretation of Gregory's ideas of 'God' to a test they have devised, and charge Gregory with inconsistency for his unwillingness to concede that his theology leads to a notion of there being three Gods.

This is how they determine Gregory to be an incoherent thinker: Gregory, they say, would accept that the instantiation of a certain thing A is the same kind of thing as another instantiation of the same thing A but these two instantiations, or for that matter all instantiations of thing A, are not the same instantiation.[43] Gregory would certainly not disagree with such an axiomatic statement. The problem is that his opponents try to make Gregory seem like he is contradicting himself by implicitly asserting that his proper definition of 'God' is as a concrete thing, or a concrete instantiation of a divine nature. Yet if 'God' is properly a concrete instantiation, and if the concrete entities which are the Father, Son, and Holy Spirit are each God, the logical implication is that they do not make up one God but presumably three Gods.[44]

The error and subtlety in the argument mounted by the opponents of Nyssen are now clear: they have taken 'God' as a synonym for 'divine person'. Once that tactical move is made, it is a foregone conclusion that Gregory is teaching that there be three Gods.

---

[42] Gregory of Nyssa, *Comm. not.* (Stramara, 383).
[43] Gregory of Nyssa, *Comm. not.* (Stramara, 387–88).
[44] Gregory of Nyssa, *Comm. not.* (Stramara, 387).

Despite the cleverness of his critics, that Gregory of Nyssa is able to provide an adequate response is testament to the lucidity of his thought. They come against him, in effect, asking why if the Father is said to be God, as well as the Son and the Holy Spirit, there should not be three Gods but one, given that when presented with the fact that Peter is a human being, as well as Paul, people are wont to conclude that there are two human beings.

Gregory highlights that Peter and Paul, for instance, are said to be two human beings out of a certain inexactness of expression.[45] In actuality, they simply constitute two concrete instantiations of the single human being or essence. This can be explained by recourse to the fact that neither Peter nor Paul are human beings by virtue of being themselves as opposed to another; that is to say, Peter is not a human being because he is Peter and not Paul. It would be plain contradiction with the statement that Paul is a human being to suggest that that is so. Instead, Peter is a human being simply because he possesses a human nature, as is Paul.

In a word, Peter is a human being *by extension* of being a bearer, or concrete instantiation, of a human nature which is indivisible because it defines the instantiations of human nature and is not defined by them. Similarly, the Father is God simply because he possesses a divine nature, which is God, as are the Son and Holy Spirit. They are God *by extension* of being a bearer, a concrete instantiation, of the divine nature. What Gregory seems to be inferring here is that it is not of perfect grammatical appropriateness to say of the Father, or the Son or the Holy Spirit, that he is God, but only he is a concrete instantiation of God, or he is 'God'. This is a fundamental limitation of the Cappadocian theory of the divine being, as this study will go on to argue.

One crucial note needs to be made: Gregory's insistence on the inadequacy of words to articulate the divine essence, while commendable, needs to be revisited. As has previously been shown, Gregory is not claiming that there is completely no way to talk about the divine nature, since he himself dilates on the subject. The point he is making is that certain terms used to speak about the divine persons are not words that express only that which human beings know by reason. Scripture does use terms that reason is able to accept on the basis of a consideration of what is written in other places.[46]

Scripture, however, also uses terms that demand not just mental examination and logic but the exercise of faith, that is, in the fact that someday those who employ the

---

[45] Gregory of Nyssa, *Comm. not.* (Stramara, 388–89).
[46] For instance, Hebrews refers to Abraham as a man of faith, and that testimony is backed up by the report in Genesis 22 concerning his act of devotion unto God.

term shall better understand what they signify. Consider the case of the revelation of the divine personal name to Moses in Exodus 3. If the view is taken that words cannot aim at signifying the fullness of divine reality without failing spectacularly at doing so for humans though not for God, thereby fulfilling a strictly formal vocative function, would it not have been impossible for the deity to introduce himself with a name which human beings could express and contemplate?

By giving Israel a name by which he could be adverted, God was declaring that his name denoted that which human beings could not, could never, fully fathom, a name to be meditated upon as much as reverenced in wonder. In the same token, human beings do not fully comprehend even those who are familiar to them, yet they address them, all the same, by human words, which they call names, showing, again, that some words are intended to be received with reason as much as faith. The name of divinity is such a word. As a matter of fact, that Gregory does not forbid the notion that human words could denote objects of ineffable wonder can be seen in the way he permits the use of adjectives to signify divine attributes, which are infinite in measure, and far exceed human comprehension.

It has been highlighted that Gregory Nyssen compares the Trinity not just to three human persons but also to one.[47] Lewis Ayres goes on to note, correctly, that in Gregory's example, the image is of a word that has a will.[48] The analogy of the human person, word, and breath does not in any way undermine that which has been said heretofore about the Gregorian or Cappadocian understanding of the being of God as qualitative, given that Gregory of Nyssa supplements his metaphors with additional personal attributes.[49]

It may be helpful to underscore the fact that Gregory Nyssen does not employ his illustrations as complete or self-sufficient analogies.[50] Often, an instance of which has just been shown, he enhances his illustrations with qualities which the objects in question do not naturally possess. The nature of the divine persons described by the objects

---

[47] L. Ayres, 'On Not Three People: The Fundamental Themes of Gregory of Nyssa's Trinitarian Theology As Seen In *To Ablabius: On Not Three Gods*', in *Re-thinking Gregory of Nyssa*, ed. S. Coakley (Malden, MA: Blackwell, 2003), p. 17.

[48] Ibid.

[49] In the case of the word, see Gregory of Nyssa, *Catech.* 1.1 (Moore, NPNF² 5:475–76); and in the case of the breath or spirit, see Gregory of Nyssa, *Catech.* 1.2 (Moore, NPNF² 5:477).

[50] Indeed, Kärkkäinen notes that Gregory of Nyssa owned to how his analogy of the three men could not fully capture the divine reality insomuch as there are only three divine persons, but there can be and are more than three human beings. V.-M. Kärkkäinen, *The Trinity: Global Perspectives* (Louisville, KY: Westminster John Knox, 2007), p. 40.

in his analogies is not, in his estimation, *less than* the specified qualities or attributes of the objects referred to in those analogies, but, in fact, *more than* them.[51] As such, one should not baulk at affirming that Gregory Nyssen did draw a parallel between the three divine persons and as many human persons; as already pointed out, this is not to assert that Gregory sees a complete equivalence between the natures of the divine persons and human ones, but, nevertheless, that the image of human persons does provide a means of attaining to a grasp, a meaningful albeit incomplete one, of the form of the divine person.

---

[51] Frederick Norris makes a similar assertion pertaining to the way in which people ought to appropriate the analogies used by Gregory Nazianzen to describe the divine nature in *Faith Gives Fullness to Reasoning*, p. 212. Giulio Maspero in 'Trinity' in *The Brill Dictionary of Gregory of Nyssa*, ed. L. F. Mateo-Seco and G. Maspero, trans. S. Cherney, VCSup 99 (Boston: Brill, 2010), pp. 754 and 759, directs attention to the way in which Gregory of Nyssa was confident that his analogies from the created order would be properly grasped in light of the right understanding of divine transcendence.

Chapter 5

Augustine of Hippo and Other Theologians

De Trinitate

The final representative to be considered at some length at least of the view that the being of God consists in a quality or a set thereof possessed equally by the Father, the Son, and the Holy Spirit is St. Augustine.[1] That Augustine has the same perspective of the divine substance as the Cappadocian Fathers is borne out in his well-known treatise on the doctrine of the Trinity: *De Trinitate*. In the middle of the work, he compares God's being with his attributes of wisdom, greatness, power, goodness and the rest.[2]

As such, Augustine's apparent rejection of the example of three gold statues, which though three share in the same substance, as a suitable analogy for understanding the Trinity must be comprehended in its proper context: that which he does not accept is not the illustration of the gold statues *per se* but the unavoidable concomitant nuance that the singular dimension is not the exclusive possession of the plural and the plural is not

---

[1] Holmes offers a variety of reasons for questioning the claim that Augustine's theology of the triune divine being differs from that of the Cappadocian Fathers. Holmes, *Quest for the Trinity*, pp. 129–31; Fairbairn, too, feels that Augustine's approach to the Trinity is similar to that of the Cappadocian Fathers. D. Fairbairn, *Life in the Trinity: An Introduction to Theology with the Help of the Church Fathers* (Downers Grove, IL: IVP Academic, 2009), pp. 44–45. Ayres holds the view that Augustine had a substantial perspective of the divine being in *Augustine and the Trinity* (Cambridge: Cambridge University Press, 2010), p. 321. See also M. R. Barnes, 'Latin Trinitarian Theology', in *The Cambridge Companion to The Trinity*, ed. P. C. Phan (Cambridge: Cambridge University Press, 2011), p. 71.

[2] Augustine of Hippo, *Trin.* 7.9–10 (Hill, WSA).

the exhaustive possessor of the quality or set thereof which is described by the singular, and, at least to him, the sense that in the material world, nature can be multiplied by increasing the number of entities under consideration.

This can be demonstrated by a juxtaposition of Augustine's pertinent comments apropos to the relationship between the nature of the Trinity and that of gold statues. Augustine says of gold statues that there is no necessary link between gold and statues[3] but that this is not the case with the Trinity, where that which is three and that which is one are necessarily related and inseparable.[4]

In sum, that with which Augustine takes issue is the incompleteness of the picture afforded by three gold statues, and, for that matter, three men. There is no outright dismissal of the illustrations as a means by which one may attain some concept of the nature of the Trinity, only a series of qualifications to the effect that when the divine persons are understood as in some way analogous to human persons—a possibility Augustine does not expressly forbid—they are not to be conceived as if they were merely members of another, albeit vastly superior, race of beings in which the divine essence is not necessarily the exclusive possession of those three members; and substance and personhood are not assigned separate dimensions of quality and personal reality respectively so that divinity is not quantified, and the divine persons in their substance add up to more than they individually are.[5]

In this regard, Augustine is not making the point that the three persons are equal in substance to one another because with infinite beings there is by definition no way to increase their qualities as Brown seems to be suggesting,[6] but for the reason that a qualitative factor is not increased via multiplication of instantiations. As admittedly and self-consciously frivolous examples, neither is the softness of a pillow augmented, nor is its materiality of cotton raised to a higher degree by placement of more pillows beside it. While in the latter case it may be possible to increase the density of cotton by combining the matter of two or more pillows, this is not so with the divine persons.

There is no way by which the substance in two or three divine persons can be combined to make for 'denser' divinity because the divine nature is represented by a

---

[3] Augustine of Hippo, *Trin.* 7.11.

[4] Ibid.

[5] Ibid. To be sure, Augustine does not appear here to suggest this solution of the Cappadocian Fathers, yet this is only because his doctrine of the divine being, which is very much in keeping with theirs and on the same theological trajectory, is, it may be said, not as well developed as theirs, at least in this particular regard.

[6] Brown, *Divine Trinity*, p. 292.

specific 'density' so that while the divine reality of the three persons is greater than a conceivable one of two or one persons, the quality of divinity is unchanged. As such, given that the 'density' of the divine substance neither increases nor decreases with the addition or subtraction of divine persons, it is fair for Augustine to highlight that the three divine persons together are equivalent to each person considered individually.

Concern about such misunderstanding may be the reason Augustine proceeds to identify other analogies of the Trinity in later sections of his work, including, most famously, his analogy of the memory, understanding, and will. The very fact that he does not scruple to consider the merits of an example drawn from mere processes of thought reveals that Augustine is not attempting in his psychological analogy to furnish a comprehensive or even general picture of the Trinity, but perhaps, more modestly, to supplement existing analogies.

To conclude the present exploration of Augustine's Trinitarian theology, it is fitting to highlight a statement which summarizes his thought on the matter to the effect that God is nature.[7] The foregoing discussion has demonstrated that the Cappadocian Fathers and Augustine of Hippo alike hold to a view of the divine being as individual makeup, orientation and action, conceiving of the divine oneness in terms of substance, will, and action, as 'God-ness'.

Other Theologians

As a matter of fact, a substantial view of the divine being was maintained through the centuries after in the theologies of Boethius, John of Damascus, Anselm of Canterbury, Richard of St. Victor, Thomas Aquinas, and John Calvin. A brief survey follows.

Boethius argues for a substantial conception of the being of God in his *Utrum Pater et Filius et Spiritus Sanctus De Divinitate substantialiter praedicentur*, relating that which is three in the divine being with the persons and that which is one with nature.[8] John of Damascus, too, conceives of the oneness of God as divine nature, in which each of the divine persons partakes fully and completely.[9]

---

[7] Augustine of Hippo, *Trin.* 5.3 (Hill, WSA; cited in Gioia, *Theological Epistemology*, 148).
[8] Boethius, *Utr. Pat.* 1.55–68 (Stewart, Rand, and Tester, LCL).
[9] John of Damascus, *Exp. fid.* 1.8 (Chase, FC). See also B. E. Daley, 'Maximus the Confessor and John of Damascus on the Trinity', in *The Holy Trinity in the Life of the Church*, ed. K. Anatolios, Holy Cross Studies in Patristic Theology and History (Grand Rapids, Mich.: Baker Academic, 2014), p. 94.

Anselm speaks of the divine persons as possessing oneness of essence and implies that divine oneness is found in and to be understood of the substance more than in any other aspect, intimating that no other oneness save qualitative or attributive oneness is to be found in the Trinity.[10] Richard of St. Victor also articulates the divine being in terms of nature.[11] According to Richard Muller, he also held a view of the divine person as a divine factor that cannot be assimilated into another.[12] Aquinas does not depart from the perspective of the divine being as makeup and orientation, writing, essentially, of a common nature among the divine persons and equating the divine being with the nature of the three persons.[13]

Recently, Stephen Holmes has contended that Aquinas thought of the category of divine personhood purely in terms of their relations of origin.[14] Apart from the objection to divine personhood signifying anything less than cognitive and conative capacity already considered and reiterated in previous sections, predicated on the fact that the fullness of the divine being subsists in each of the three divine persons, it is unclear how such an assertion might withstand the theological implication of certain statements in the *Summa Theologiae* to the same effect.

In discussing whether the idea of personhood in God denotes relation, Aquinas says, among other things, that the three persons of the godhead are independently existing relations.[15] Aquinas proceeds with an exposition of the connection between divine personhood and relation.[16] Even as Holmes recognizes the Thomistic application of the concept of subsistence to the divine persons in defining them as subsistent relations, he seems to neglect the import of the adjective to place undue, nearly exclusive, stress on the noun. Notice that he interprets Thomas as completely equating divine personhood with divine relation rather than essence. While Aquinas himself rejects as unsatisfactory the notion that divine personhood is to be equated with the divine essence, he does not

---

[10] Anselm of Canterbury, *Mon.* 1.44 (Deane, OCC).

[11] Richard of St. Victor, *Trin.* 4.9 (Angelici).

[12] R. A. Muller, *The Triunity of God*, vol. 4 of *Post-Reformation Reformed Dogmatics: The Rise and Development of Reformed Orthodoxy, ca. 1520 to ca. 1725* (Grand Rapids, MI: Baker Academic, 2002), p. 34.

[13] Thomas Aquinas, *ST* 39.2 (Fathers of the English Dominican Province).

[14] S. R. Holmes, 'Trinitarian Action and Inseparable Operations: Some Historical and Dogmatic Reflections', in *Advancing Trinitarian Theology: Explorations in Constructive Dogmatics*, ed. O. D. Crisp and F. Sanders, Los Angeles Theology Conference (Grand Rapids, MI: Zondervan, 2014), p. 69.

[15] Thomas Aquinas, *ST* 29.4 and 29.2 (Fathers of the English Dominican Province).

[16] Ibid., 29.4.

completely do away with the idea of the divine essence in defining the divine person. In point of fact, he avers that divine personhood expresses the divine nature in secondary sense and relation in a primary manner.[17]

All told, Aquinas appears to be of the opinion that the distinctive and internally differentiating relations in the divine being have actual existence. Like the concept of hypostasis in the Cappadocian Fathers earlier examined, the idea of subsistent relations signifies the divine essence instantiated. This begs the question of the manner and form of instantiation in the case of the divine persons. There may be a hint of a solution in Aquinas' earlier statement that divine fatherhood is identical with the Father.

Is it necessary to assume that Aquinas is relativizing divine personhood; that is, turning God the Father into a notion or relation of divine paternity? Could Aquinas be here redefining the concept of divine relations in ontological terms; that is, turning the notion or relation of divine paternity into the cognitive and conative center that God the Father is and equating the two? In other words, is Aquinas assuming knowledge of relation, and striving for a definition, or redefinition, of the personhood of the Father? Or is he assuming knowledge of the personhood of the Father, and striving for a definition of relation?

That which is indisputable is that Aquinas is seeking to establish the answer to the question he has posed for himself: Do person and relation share a single meaning? Clearly, Aquinas is not simply trying to define divine personhood, but to determine if there is a semantic equivalence between the concepts of divine personhood and divine relation. On the assumption that Aquinas has satisfactorily addressed his own concern, an important element appears to be missing: the definition of divine relation, crucial to answering the question.

Both possibilities need to be tested for logical coherence. If Aquinas were trying to relativize the person of the Father, and turn it into a relation, this would not be consistent with his definition of the divine person as subsistent relation, and therefore possessing the ability to exist independently, since relations, as conventionally understood, do not have an independent existence.[18] This problem does not occur on the view that Aquinas is trying to ontologize the relation of the Father to the Son.

---

[17] Ibid.

[18] Paul Fiddes would disagree, though not without sparking controversy. See T. H. McCall, 'Relational Trinity: Radical Perspective: Response to Paul S. Fiddes', in *Two Views on the Doctrine of the Trinity*, ed. J. S. Sexton and S. N. Gundry, Counterpoints (Grand Rapids, MI: Zondervan, 2014), pp. 199–200. Granted that there is a technical possibility of a divine relation having an

Moreover, a closer reading yields an implicit exposition of relation and personhood. After highlighting that person as applied to human beings signifies the whole individual, Aquinas immediately goes on to equate a string of terms with the significations of difference, relation, nature, and person in regard to the divine being. That he identifies relation and personhood with the divine essence is most important for the present discussion, because in so doing he furnishes the content of divine relation and personhood. Like the human person, the divine person is not a meaningless formal concept but bears signification.

Saying that the divine person is the divine essence is simply another way of affirming one of the core tenets of Trinitarian doctrine: that the Father is God, the Son is God, and the Holy Spirit is God.[19] On this reading, the statement that divine fatherhood is identical with the Father makes perfect sense as an explanation and redefinition of divine relation following the definition of the divine person, to which relation is equated.[20] Consequently, there is a firm basis for comprehending the Thomistic doctrine of divine personhood as possessing the fullness of the divine being, and thereby cognitive and conative, being more than relations.[21]

According to C. Welch, Aquinas and also John Calvin conceived of God in terms of essence.[22]

---

independent existence, if Aquinas were trying to propagate this kind of thinking, he would be remiss in not saying more about it and anticipating objections.

[19] Muller, *Triunity of God*, p. 48.

[20] Aquinas explicitly equates the relations of both Father and Son to each other with their persons, in *ST* 40.2 (Fathers of the English Dominican Province).

[21] D. F. Kelly, *The God Who Is: The Holy Trinity*, vol. 1 of *Systematic Theology: Grounded in Holy Scripture and Understood in the Light of the Church* (Ross-shire, Scotland: Mentor, 2008), pp. 498–99.

[22] C. Welch, *The Trinity in Contemporary Theology* (London: SCM, 1953), pp. 190–91 (cited by Gunton, *Becoming and Being: The Doctrine of God in Charles Hartshorne and Karl Barth*, 2nd ed. [London: SCM, 2001], p. 142).

Part 2

Theologians of 'God-ity'

After the qualitative focus on the divine being, the next watershed in thinking about the same would be an emphasis on being as relational dynamic.

Whereas theologians of 'God-ness' addressed the aspects of individual makeup, orientation and action and conceived of God as comprising three ontologically independent divine persons with the same makeup, will, purpose, and action, theologians of 'God-ity' articulated a concept of the divine being in relational terms with an image of the divine reality as three ontologically independent but relationally interdependent divine persons with the same makeup, will, purpose, and action.

This new perspective, propagated by theologians like J. D. Zizioulas, C. E. Gunton, and T. A. Smail, involves the conversion of the concept of interdependence into an ontological idea.[1]

---

[1] Another theologian who espouses the idea of the divine being as relationship is David Cunningham, who uses the concept of the mutual participation of the divine persons in each other's lives to develop a theory of God in relational terms in *These Three Are One: The Practice of Trinitarian Theology*, Challenges in Contemporary Theology (Malden, MA: Blackwell, 1998), pp. 165, 168–69.

Chapter 6

John D. Zizioulas, Colin E. Gunton, and Thomas A. Smail

John D. Zizioulas

An influential and innovative interpreter of the Trinitarian theology of the Cappadocian Fathers,[1] the titular Eastern Orthodox metropolitan bishop John Zizioulas is of the opinion that being cannot be understood apart from the fellowship of persons. God's is no exception.[2] In so asserting, Zizioulas is not simply aiming at a restoration of the concept of the triple personhood of God to a position of emphasis which rightfully belongs to it as much as such belongs to the divine substance in a perception of doctrinal imbalance which he has.

This he makes clear by his counter-assertion that rather than substance, the triple personhood of God, as a key ontological factor,[3] should take theological precedence in the idea of the divine reality seeing that the content of the divine being is filled by relationship.[4] Evidently, Zizioulas is here undertaking nothing less than a redefinition of the

---

[1] M. Volf, *After Our Likeness: The Church as the Image of the Trinity*, Sacra Doctrina (Grand Rapids, MI: Eerdmans, 1998), pp. 73–75.

[2] J. D. Zizioulas, *Being as Communion: Studies in Personhood and the Church*, CGT 4 (Crestwood, NY: St. Vladimir's Seminary Press, 1985), p. 17.

[3] Ibid.

[4] Ibid.

concept of the divine essence in terms of interpersonal dynamic[5] albeit he thinks it was a discovery of the church fathers.[6]

For Zizioulas, the oneness of God is not safeguarded by the common divine essence as much as by the person of the Father as origin, the constitutive factor or element, of the fellowship of the godhead, and therefore, since fellowship forms being, the ontologically constitutive element.[7] The implication of the assertion of Zizioulas concerning the divine substance is monumental: within less than two pages he has enunciated what is possibly an original vision of the essence of God, as relationship.

This radical proposal may be better understood in light of Zizioulas' view of personhood. He seems strongly to suggest that everything that makes someone a person is constituted and sustained by, presumably, regular interaction with other persons,[8] but the identity thereby obtained is not an independently guaranteed possession of its holder, but contingent on continued social engagement with the other. Consequently, Zizioulas is able to speak of an ontological effect death has on a person.[9] As a matter of fact, Zizioulas would proceed in another place to infer that those who lose all their relationships can only be headed toward non-existence; that is, death.[10] His claim that human persons lose their psychological and social ability and wellness in isolation from other people is applied, without any qualification whatsoever, to the divine persons.[11]

The salient point is as follows: just as a human person so relies on social intercourse for socio-psychological wellbeing that without relationships, Zizioulas implies, they will lose their personhood, so the divine persons so rely on one another's presence for their socio-psychological wellbeing that if the Father did not exist, for all intents and purposes the Son as Son would not exist either; that is, the Son would not exist as a person, but as something far poorer, and unworthy of the name of the Son, which indicates a personal distinction within the Godhead.

---

[5] As is also observed in T. H. McCall, *Which Trinity? Whose Monotheism? Philosophical and Systematic Theologians on the Metaphysics of Trinitarian Theology* (Grand Rapids, MI: William B. Eerdmans, 2010), pp. 190–92.

[6] Zizioulas, *Being as Communion*, p. 17.

[7] Ibid., pp. 17–18.

[8] J. D. Zizioulas, 'Human Capacity and Human Incapacity: A Theological Exploration of Personhood', in *SJT* 28, no. 5 (October 1975), pp. 407–8; idem., *Lectures in Christian Dogmatics* (London: T&T Clark, 2008), p. 26.

[9] Zizioulas, *Lectures in Christian Dogmatics*, p. 26.

[10] Idem., *Lectures in Christian Dogmatics*, p. 53

[11] Ibid., pp. 26, 53; cf. Zizioulas, 'Human Capacity and Human Incapacity', pp. 435–36.

In itself, the recognition that the personhoods of the Father, Son, and Holy Spirit are mutually constituted on the basis of a shared need for fellowship and communion is sufficient to establish the proposition that the being of God, made up as it is of the Father, Son, and Holy Spirit as no less than persons, consists in the fellowship of the divine persons. The discussion is superficially complicated by Zizioulas' assertion, in his opinion following the Greek fathers, that the Father is the one God.[12] This, however, must be comprehended through the grid of his insistence that the Father as person and thus the divine being itself is fundamentally dependent on the existence of the Son and Holy Spirit, each being sustained socio-psychologically by the others.

In this way, to speak of the divine being, derivatively, since the being of God, properly speaking, refers to divine fellowship, as the Father in the glory of his personhood is really to speak of the divine being as Father, Son, and Holy Spirit in relationship. What Zizioulas may be attempting to convey is that the Father alone is the exalted actualization and realization of the divine being as substance, while the actual self-subsisting, independently existing divine being, in an acquired sense, comprises the Father, Son, and Holy Spirit in communion. This is how one might make sense of his double reference to God as relationship and as the Father.[13]

By adverting to the Father as solely possessing the distinct honor of being addressed as 'God', at the same time that he proffers the idea of the divine being as fellowship, Zizioulas presents two complementary ways of understanding the unity of God, the former of which tries to do justice to the Old Testament concept of God as single personal being. Unfortunately this solution runs into a critical problem of its own. For one, it begs the question of why the Son and Holy Spirit are not similarly honored with the title of deity. Due to the risk of being perceived to detract from the deity of the Son and the Holy Spirit, this option must be rejected outright.

If the Cappadocian Fathers and Augustine developed a doctrine of the divine being as reality of individual personal quality and ability, Zizioulas has boldly and creatively recast it as reality of interpersonal relationship.[14] In the final analysis, there may be no real need to force a choice between the options, which seem to describe the being of God from different angles. The one looks at the divine substance from the standpoint of

---

[12] Zizioulas, *Lectures in Christian Dogmatics*, p. 68.

[13] Ibid.

[14] See Tim Chester's summary of Zizioulas' thesis in *Being as Communion* in *Delighting in the Trinity: Why Father, Son and Spirit are Good News*, 2nd ed. (Surrey, UK: The Good Book, 2010), p. 117. Veli-Matti Kärkkäinen paraphrases Zizioulas' theology in *The Trinity: Global Perspectives* (Louisville, KY: Westminster John Knox, 2007), p. 92.

character and attributes, reflecting a distinctively Greek outlook[15] and the monarchial or imperial context in which the patristic theologians wrote; the other attempts to speak of the being of God through the lens of a modern world—and its philosophies[16]—which has seen and continues to see the fall of authoritarian regimes, in fits and starts though it be, and the attendant rise of popular democracies and entry into the mainstream, particularly with the advent of telecommunications, air travel, and the internet and the expansion of educational and professional opportunities, of the recognition that no person, family, community, society or even continent exists in a vacuum, disconnected from the rest of the world.

Amid the changes, it is imperative to maintain a perspective which takes holistic account of the reality of God. As much as the divine being has to do with relational interaction and the economy of God itself may indeed be understood in terms of the divine relationship with creation, as Zizioulas might contend, discussion of the personal qualities of the Father, the Son, and the Holy Spirit cannot be marginalized without threatening the basic unit of fellowship, which remains the individual person.

Zizioulas seems to be cognizant of this danger and, in response, introduces the idea of the person of the Father as the underlying source of divine fellowship.[17] Ultimately, however, a watertight system with a radical stress on fellowship which does not admit of due consideration of individual character can only collapse upon itself. To maintain the conviction that fellowship is the sine qua non of being and substance is to impugn even the usefulness of the notion of the Father as the constitutive factor in the Trinity. In the end, the Father, and for that matter, the Son and the Holy Spirit, are only valuable insofar as they constitute a fellowship. Inescapably, the value of the individual person is downplayed.

Accordingly, Zizioulas *cannot* of necessity be asserting complete dominance of the relational paradigm of the divine being to the exclusion of any other sense of existence in the godhead. Indeed, he does not, indicating the relative nature of his thesis in noting how the Greek church fathers did not think of substance save in its personal instantia-

---

[15] C. M. Bowra, *Classical Greece*, Great Ages of Man: A History of the World's Cultures (Amsterdam: Time-Life International (Nederland), 1965), pp. 11–17.

[16] As noted in L. Turcescu, '"Person" versus "Individual", and Other Modern Misreadings of Gregory of Nyssa', in *Re-thinking Gregory of Nyssa*, ed. S. Coakley (Malden, MA: Blackwell, 2003), pp. 97–109. See also K. Anatolios, 'Personhood, Communion, and the Trinity in Some Patristic Texts', in *The Holy Trinity in the Life of the Church*, Holy Cross Studies in Patristic Theology and History, ed. K. Anatolios (Grand Rapids, MI: Baker Academic, 2014), pp. 147–49.

[17] Zizioulas, *Being as Communion*, pp. 17–18.

tions, by which, in acknowledging the substance that resides in the individual person, he acknowledges that being continues to have the sense of individual quality.[18]

In all likelihood, Zizioulas is wishing to complement the substance or individual-oriented understanding of the being of God by furnishing a relational category as an overarching framework. On this view, perhaps, the divine persons each have an ontological existence in themselves, but this ontological existence is not to be equated with divine being or the fullness of divine personhood, which can only be attained in relationship and fellowship.[19] In this connection, Volf draws a helpful distinction in Zizioulas' theology between the divine persons giving rise to and affecting one another.[20]

It has seemly been demonstrated that Zizioulas shares a similar if not common understanding of the divine being with Karl Barth. If Barth, argues Paul Collins, espouses a conception of the being of God as act and event,[21] Zizioulas thinks in similar terms.[22] Insomuch as this assertion clashes with the claim noted in this study that the concepts of the divine being espoused by Barth and Zizioulas are to be distinguished, the thesis proposed by Collins is worth a second and closer look.

Since the fundamental disagreement does not lie primarily with the understanding of Barth, attention will be given solely to that of Zizioulas. Collins highlights the latter's use of an expression of fellowship as event in the context of his discussion of the divine being and how, as he sees it, St. Athanasius and the Cappadocian Fathers have conceptualized it.[23] In the opinion of this writer, he makes two interpretive moves which can be questioned.

A first is that Collins seems to think that Zizioulas equates the relations of origin in the divine being with the fellowship of which Zizioulas says that it constitutes the being of God.[24] This cannot be true, for the divine relations of origin, whether conceived on-

---

[18] Ibid., pp. 41–42, n. 37.

[19] A. Papanikolaou, 'Sophia, Apophasis, and Communion: the Trinity in Contemporary Orthodox Theology', in *The Cambridge Companion to The Trinity*, ed. P. C. Phan (Cambridge: Cambridge University Press, 2011), pp. 251–52.

[20] Volf, *After Our Likeness*, pp. 79–80.

[21] P. M. Collins, *Trinitarian Theology: West and East: Karl Barth, the Cappadocian Fathers, and John Zizioulas* (Oxford: Oxford University Press, 2001), pp. 174, 176.

[22] Ibid., p. 182.

[23] Ibid., pp. 177–83, which cites use of the expression describing fellowship as event in Zizioulas, *Being as Communion*, pp. 17–18.

[24] Collins, *Trinitarian Theology*, pp. 181–82.

tologically[25] or relationally,[26] are logically prior to relationship of any sort. As such, they cannot be absolutely identified one with the other but are to be seen as distinct, albeit the two are intimately related, even inseparable.

The second assumption of Collins' is that Zizioulas uses the expression that describes fellowship as event in reference to the fellowship of the divine persons that comprises the divine being.[27] This is rendered implausible by his measured phraseology. Rather than positing an exact identity between fellowship as event and the divine being, Zizioulas introduces an idea of a mediating relation of efficient causation.

It is timely here to consider the two places cited by Collins in which Zizioulas employs the expression. In a first,[28] it is to be noted that Zizioulas is addressing the issue of the *existence* of God or the *fact* of his being, rather than that of the *being* of God or the *nature* of his being. In essence, he is asserting that on one level, namely, that of efficient causation within the Godhead, fellowship in the form of the act of the causation by the Father of the Son and the Holy Spirit, an event which is also given the name of fellowship in recognition of its ontological implication, on this level, fellowship as event accounts for the *fact* of the being of God. On another, it cannot be gainsaid that Zizioulas articulates the divine being in terms of the fellowship that characterizes the life of the three divine persons.

In another passage in which Zizioulas utilizes the concept of fellowship as event[29], although Zizioulas avers that the divine being is the result of the Father and that the being of God is from the Father as one who acknowledges his being by his eternal causation of the Son and the Holy Spirit, he does not here define the divine being in terms of the concept of fellowship as event to which he adverts, given that this very concept is the precondition for the emergence or production of the divine being, by the agency of the Father.

What of an undeniably clear statement in Zizioulas to the effect that the divine being amounts to an act of fellowship?[30] In its immediate context,[31] it appears that Ziziou-

---

[25] The Father or Son or Holy Spirit needs first to exist before they may relate with one another; thus, the fact of existence precedes, logically, the fact of relationship.

[26] The Father or Son or Holy Spirit needs first his distinctive self-identity as Father, Son, or Holy Spirit before there is a cause and animus to relate one with another; thus, the fact of self-identity precedes, logically, the fact of relationship.

[27] Collins, *Trinitarian Theology*, p. 182.

[28] Zizioulas, *Being as Communion*, p. 17, cited in Collins, *Trinitarian Theology*, p. 178.

[29] Zizioulas, *Being as Communion*, p. 18, cited in Collins, *Trinitarian Theology*, p. 179.

[30] Zizioulas, *Being as Communion*, p. 44.

las is giving the divine being new significance as an act of fellowship. This, however, would be to contradict his earlier definition of the being of God simply as fellowship. The distinction is more than a subtle one of merely rarefied importance. If fellowship is understood as an act or event, the emphasis is placed on the fact of its occurrence and the nature of its development, giving the concept an impersonal and purely formal meaning; on the other hand, understood as a collective entity, fellowship encapsulates the ideas of a group comprising numerous members, connected formally but also interpersonally, and having a common identity and goals.

In other words, fellowship conceived as act or event excludes the significations of personhood and personal relationship, whereas fellowship conceived as a collective entity encompasses the personal and interpersonal dimensions. For this reason, it is imperative to insist on what may be seen as an overly particular reading of the intent of Zizioulas as postulating a concept of the divine being not in terms of fellowship as act or event, but as fellowship, tout court.[32]

To return to the argument, in view of the semantic conflict between the ideas of the divine being as event of fellowship, and as fellowship, one must opt in favor of the signification which is supported by a wider reading of the text, which this study has clearly identified. The statement in question itself is amenable to an alternate interpretation in light of the fact that it is preceded by another, which highlights God's decision involving the being of God as the Father.

Arguably, this statement is incomprehensible apart from an apprehension of the divine being in terms of fellowship as collective entity. How could God choose to be the Father, or how might one consider God only as Father, unless the divine being comprises the three persons of the Father, the Son, and the Holy Spirit which can be analyzed, to a certain extent, individually as well as collectively? In this way, the statement to the effect that the divine being amounts to fellowship as act is to be grasped as shorthand for the being of God as Father amounts to fellowship as act in that through 'begetting' the Son and 'bringing forth' the Holy Spirit, the Father acknowledges his identity[33]; it is not to be understood as equating the being of God with an act of fellowship.[34]

---

[31] Ibid.
[32] Zizioulas, *Lectures in Christian Dogmatics*, p. 53.
[33] Zizioulas, *Being as Communion*, p. 18.
[34] While Zizioulas' conception of the divine being only makes sense with an understanding of the divine person as cognitive and conative centers of consciousness, since it is only in that way that the persons may be in communion one with another, those who might seek a statement from Zizioulas concerning his view on divine personhood are requested to consult his paper

Also emphasizing the centrality of the relational aspect of the divine being is C. E. Gunton, the next theologian whose understanding of the being of God is to be reviewed and discussed.

Colin E. Gunton

Building on an insight appertaining to the apprehension of the divine being, Colin Gunton declares in no uncertain terms that the being of God is no more and no less than the sum total of the relations and interaction between the persons of the Father, the Son, and the Holy Spirit. He develops his Trinitarian doctrine on the basis of a notion of a relational interdependence of persons, whether divine or human.[35]

Gunton distinguishes his doctrine of the divine being from that of earlier theologians.[36] In his reading of the Cappadocians, he perceives an overturning of a traditional way of thinking about the being of God.[37] According to Gunton in two contexts, the fourth century architects of the Trinitarian doctrine discovered that the being of God is to be equated with the relationship between the divine persons.[38]

In both contexts he adduces a statement made by either Basil or his brother Gregory Nyssen as evidence that the Cappadocian Fathers espoused the view that the divine being is equivalent to the interpersonal dynamic between the three divine persons. This apparent affirmation is found in the fourth paragraph of the thirty-eighth epistle ascribed to Basil of Caesarea in the Benedictine arrangement in Migne's Patrologia Graeca: τινα συνεχῆ καὶ ἀδιάσπαστον κοινωνίαν ἐν αὐτοῖς θεωρεῖσθαι.

In Gunton's interpretation, citing an English translation, of the statement it highlights God as a fellowship.[39] However, understood in its context, the phrase does not equate the divine substance to interpersonal relations. Arguably, it does not even assert

---

'Human Capacity and Human Incapacity', at pp. 410, 447, for there he presents God as the only being who is really personal and speaks also of human personhood as the *imago Dei*.

[35] C. E. Gunton, *Father, Son and Holy Spirit: Essays Toward a Fully Trinitarian Theology* (London: T&T Clark, 2003), pp. 14, 16; idem., *Act and Being: Towards a Theology of the Divine Attributes* (Grand Rapids, MI: William B. Eerdmans, 2003), p. 122.

[36] Gunton, *Promise of Trinitarian Theology*, pp. 8–11.

[37] Ibid.

[38] Ibid.; idem., *The Christian Faith: An Introduction to Christian Doctrine* (Malden, MA: Blackwell, 2002), pp. 186–87.

[39] M. Wiles and M. Santer, eds, *Documents in Early Christian Thought* (Cambridge: Cambridge University Press, 1975), pp. 34–35 (cited by C. E. Gunton, *Promise of Trinitarian Theology*, p. 10).

anything about how the divine persons are persons in community in the godhead. Rather than conflating the concepts of substance and relation, the writer is affirming the unity of the divine nature that is present in the three persons.[40]

Consequently, it may make better sense to render κοινωνίαν in the phrase in question as 'association', applied to divine attributes, rather than a word like 'fellowship', applied to the relations of the divine persons, to bring out the idea that the complete identity of the substance of the three divine persons is being contrasted with their distinctive relations with one another. By being without break and undisrupted the writer is referring to the identity or sameness of the divine attributes whereby there is no necessity for a break in thought in considering one divine person to consider another since the sighting of one is tantamount to the sighting of the second or the third, the divine persons being exactly the same in their nature, character, makeup and qualities.

This point may be substantiated by noting that the writer proceeds to introduce the analogy of the rainbow already discussed previously. To recapitulate, the purpose of that example is to establish that considered individually or absolutely, there is no difference between the divine persons. There is utterly no distinction to be made in contemplation that focuses on any one divine person concerning the nature and actions of that person. Indeed, any naked creaturely contemplation of the divine is unable to differentiate between the persons, since the difference between them is a purely relational one to which solely the divine persons themselves are privy.[41]

It is possible to differentiate between human persons simply because they have different physical bodies which constitute the loci of their activity and relations. In the case of God, however, there is no material substance by which an observer may distinguish between the persons of the Father, the Son, and the Holy Spirit. Given that the only access human beings have to the knowledge of the essence of God is through his operation, in which the effort of the divine persons is indistinguishable, as well as the incarnation of the Son, all that human beings are able to gather from this testimony of experience is what the Father, the Son, and the Holy Spirit are like; it is not given, however, to humans to differentiate between the three divine persons, since that difference is not a matter of being but relation.

---

[40] Basil of Caesarea, *Ep.* 38.4 (Deferrari, LCL), corresponding to LCL 190:207, 209, 211.

[41] John Behr takes the same view of the interpretation of κοινωνίαν in *The Nicene Faith*, vol. 2 of *The Formation of Christian Theology* (Crestwood, NY: St. Vladimir's Seminary Press, 2004), 2:420–23. He highlights an additional support from another work of the writer, whom he takes to be Gregory of Nyssa in *Against Eunomius* 3.1; GNO 1.2, p. 36.

To be sure, the incarnation of the Son has made it possible to 'see' the second person of the Trinity and therefore to 'distinguish' Him from the first and third persons, and the divine persons may manifest themselves in distinctive forms, yet in the bareness of the being of God, there is no way for an external observer[42] to tell one divine person from another until they relate with one another.

In following the tack of Zizioulas, Gunton exposes himself to the same criticism made about the former. Once again, there is no relationship without individuals because there is no relational capacity without concrete persons. As such, more than anything else, the theology of divine being as relational reality should be built upon the same as the reality of character and ability.

The conceptualization of the divine substance or being in terms of relationships shared by the divine persons does not have to be at variance with that in terms of individual makeup or composition. Likewise, the conception of God as a complex of interaction, rooted in the fact and governing principle that the promise or potential of each divine person is ineluctably and eternally tied to the presence and wellbeing of the others, with a meaning analogous to that of the concept of a single 'humanity', does not have to be at odds with that as substance. The meaning of the divine being need not be exhausted by the idea of perfect community, mutuality, and solidarity as integral to who God is.

Indeed, the one could be named the qualitative aspect of the being of God, which is present in the divine persons individually, while the other might be called the relational aspect of the divine, which is present in the divine persons collectively. In both cases it might be better to understand the name of God in the same way that the idea of divinity is comprehended, not as pointing to a single, personal reality but to an abstraction, a quality of a personal entity or group thereof. The only distinction is this: divinity when applied to the individual divine person is described as 'God-ness' or the possession by an individual person of that which makes one divine, whereas when applied collectively to the three divine persons, it is understood as 'God-ity' or the sum total of the vibrant, selfless, and mutually beneficial relations between the persons in the godhead.

T. A. Smail applies insights about the connection between personhood or selfhood and relationship to the practical implication of the doctrine of the Trinity for human attitude and conduct.

---

[42] Assuming that one is able to perceive the being of God in its essence.

Thomas A. Smail

Another proponent of the idea of the divine being as interpersonal relation is Thomas Smail. He speaks about a mutual relational necessity of the three divine persons, and how it is only in relation with one another that they may form a community that bears the name of God.[43] In a work exploring the practical implications of the doctrine of the Trinity for relations between human persons, he highlights the relational dependence of persons on the communities of which they are part, implicitly suggesting that a similar state of affairs obtains with the Trinity.

Smail taps on the insights of W. Pannenberg, J. Baillie, as well as indigenous African philosophy in developing his idea.[44] Comparing interpersonal personal development to self-development which transpires within a professional setting, he highlights, paraphrasing the insight of W. Pannenberg, that the element of receiving and giving, integral to the formation of the person, is present as early as birth.[45] Not only does a baby depend physically on the care of its mother, but emotionally and psychologically as well. The baby does not have everything in itself to become a complete human person short of sustenance but is taught by its mother about its dependence on other persons.[46]

Smail summarizes the implications of the finding by noting that the self comes into existence only in relation to other persons.[47] Contrary to the understanding that human beings begin as individuals, the fact is that people begin in relationship, by which they develop a sense of self-awareness.[48] Conversely, if such person-forming love is denied a baby, it cannot become a full person.[49] Smail quotes the words of D. Tutu on the indigenous African concept of *ubuntu*, concerning what makes human beings human, expressing a similar idea.[50] Such an idea of human personhood reflects the personhood of the

---

[43] T. A. Smail, *Like Father, Like Son: The Trinity Imaged in Our Humanity* (Milton Keynes, UK: Paternoster, 2005), pp. 137–41, 147–50.
[44] Ibid.
[45] Ibid.
[46] Ibid.
[47] Ibid.
[48] Ibid.
[49] Ibid.
[50] D. Tutu, 'Restoring Justice', in *The Tablet* (2004), p. 14 (cited by T. A. Smail, *Like Father, Like Son: The Trinity Imaged in Our Humanity* [Milton Keynes, UK: Paternoster, 2005], p. 139).

Father, the Son, and the Holy Spirit[51] and reflects the relationships between the divine persons.[52]

Unlike Gunton, Smail does not seem to be of the view that relational dynamic must supplant individuality as an ontological category in regard to the being of God, seeing that he approvingly cites Tutu where the latter does not omit to highlight the symbiotic connection between the two.[53]

---

[51] Smail, *Like Father, Like Son*, pp. 137–41, 147–50.
[52] Ibid.
[53] Tutu, 'Restoring Justice', p. 14 (cited by Smail, *Like Father, Like Son*, p. 139).

Part 3

A Proposal

Theologians of the past have done much to illuminate the doctrine of the Trinity by means of perspectives of the divine being as substance and relational dynamic. Although the three in God has been amply attested to in terms of real personhood, the idea of God as a single personal being is not similarly affirmed. This is where a third logical move is necessary, in which the divine being and divine personhood are brought together as one, so that the Father, the Son, and the Holy Spirit, are no longer 'God' only by derivation—insomuch as they individually possess the divine substance or divine relationship—but each of them directly and immediately God, yet without any intimation of there being three Gods.

Chapter 7

Finding a Place for the One in the Three: The Procrustean Bed of Trinitarian Theology

There is a sense in which one half of the oft-repeated paradigm of Théodore de Régnon, the statement about how Greek theology analyzes the triune nature of God with triple personhood as a starting point,[1] describes the general development of the doctrine of the Trinity as a whole, at least from the standpoint of the history of the concept of the divine being.

In articulating their understanding of the triune being of God, key theologians have embraced the reality of the three divine persons with unstinting alacrity and in an uncompromising way. The same cannot be said of their handling of the reality of the ontological oneness of God, which they seem quite willing to jettison in favor of new ideas of what it means to speak of God as one. Comparisons by the Cappadocian Fathers and Augustine of the divine persons with human ones, balanced with little if any affirmation of the ontology of the oneness of God, bear witness to this.

A Problem Unresolved

Yet an understanding of God as one that is anything but ontological is not necessarily scripturally defensible, especially with passages like Isa. 45:5 which records the direct

---

[1] M. R. Barnes, 'Augustine in Contemporary Trinitarian Theology', *TS* 56 (1995), pp. 237–38.

speech of a single speaker who identifies himself by the personal name of God, and declares that he alone is God.[2] Even if a council, assembly or nation may be spoken of by others using singular pronouns, predicative words, and verbs, it is not common for these bodies to refer to themselves in direct speech using the first person pronoun. There remains a problem and challenge of enunciating a concept of the being of God that takes into account his ontological oneness as well as the reality, which is no less substantial, of the divine persons.

Some writers have taken seriously the single and personal portrayal of God; among them, Christopher Seitz, Donald Fairbairn and Thomas Smail have claimed that the God of the Old Testament refers to the Father.[3] Such an assertion does not obviate the logical difficulty of the Trinitarian doctrine. While the divine self-revelation is thus placed in a larger doctrinal perspective, the same does not admit of mere domestication since it is attended by the fact that the one who speaks, God, claims to be the only divine entity.

According to one interpretation, early theologians from both East and West[4] have attempted to resolve this issue by appealing to an idea of a monarchy of the Father, which emphasizes the status of the Father as the divine being and ground and source of the deity of the Son and the Holy Spirit and distinguishes the Father from the other two divine persons as a more primal divinity than the two entities with derived divine na-

---

[2] If this is so, one has reason to ask on what grounds it might be said, as William Lane Craig has suggested, that the Father, Son, and Holy Spirit are divine in the sense that they are portions of the Trinity. Quite clearly, this is not the sense in which God is used in Isa. 45:5. If it were, if the speaker meant simply that he is one part of the divine being, he would not be telling the truth in claiming to be the only God since there are two other portions to the Godhead, as 'divine' as he is, and as deserving of the title of God. What the speaker probably means is that he is the one and only God in the strongest possible way; the divine being in all its fullness. As a result, assertions such as made by Craig to the effect that Scripture does not uphold a view of divine simplicity and the fullness of divinity of each person even in clear opposition to the Athanasian Creed, cannot stand, and it must be highlighted that his ensuing model of a Trinitarian monotheism is not exegetically and theologically viable. Craig, 'Toward a Tenable Social Trinitarianism', pp. 94–99.

[3] Seitz refers to the God in the Old Testament as the Father Jesus addressed. C. R. Seitz, *Word Without End: The Old Testament as Abiding Theological Witness* (Grand Rapids, MI: William B. Eerdmans, 1998), p. 258; Fairbairn, *Life in the Trinity*, p. 43; T. A. Smail, *Like Father, Like Son: The Trinity Imaged in Our Humanity* (Milton Keynes, UK: Paternoster, 2005), p. 160. An opposing view, that YHWH refers to the Trinity, is adopted by Diekamp. D. Coffey, *Deus Trinitas: The Doctrine of the Triune God* (New York: Oxford University Press, 1999), p. 70.

[4] So Tertullian, Origen, and Eusebius of Caesarea according to Prestige in *God in Patristic Thought* (Eugene, OR: Wipf & Stock, 2008), pp. 98–99, 132–33, 142–45. See also Zachhuber, 'Gregory of Nyssa on Universals', p. 85.

tures.⁵ This need not be thought of as positing any ontological superiority or inferiority within the Godhead for the reason that a non-temporal relational structural scheme might be applied as will be done in the proposal around which this study has been constructed.

The weakness, nevertheless, of this conception of the divine being as the person of the Father is that it raises the question of the nature of the relationship between the single and triple factors in God. Assuming, for the sake of argument, that the Father were separated from the Son and the Holy Spirit. In such a hypothetical situation, though the Father would remain in existence, the Son and the Holy Spirit would blink out of existence on account of the fact that their realities depend on that of the Father. As such, the three personal distinctions in the Godhead are not all fundamentally related to the divine being given that the divine being as the person of the Father is capable of an existence independent of the Son and the Holy Spirit.

This conception is also quite unable to cope with the issue of how if there is no ontological distinction between the Father, the Son, and the Holy Spirit, the exclusive ascription to the Father of the name of God could be maintained without prejudice to the acceptance of the deity of the other two divine persons.⁶ Be that as it may, it is still necessary to address the question of how the Old Testament could refer to the Father as the one true God, if in fact it does, without denying or undermining the deity of the Son and the Holy Spirit.

---

⁵ The Cappadocians do discuss the divine monarchy, but not one understood in the sense of the Father being absolute deity and the Son and the Spirit sharing in His divinity. This latter conception, which effectively makes the Father ontologically independent, and the Son and Spirit ontologically dependent on the Father and therefore ontologically inferior to Him, is in contradiction with the Cappadocians' profession regarding the ontological equality of the three divine persons, as Torrance also notes. When the Cappadocians write about causal relations within the Trinity as Torrance describes them, they are not speaking of 'cause' in an ontological sense but as a synonym for the role of the Father in relation to the Son and Holy Spirit, or the roles of the Father and the Son in relation to the Holy Spirit; these being roles which the three divine persons have in eternity assumed for themselves. For a fuller discussion, see the section on the theology of Gregory Nyssen. T. F. Torrance, *The Christian Doctrine of God: One Being, Three Persons* (London: T&T Clark, 1996), p. 182; idem., *The Trinitarian Faith: The Evangelical Theology of the Ancient Catholic Church* (London: T&T Clark, 1991), pp. 317–18.

⁶ George Prestige recognizes this difficulty and classes the theory of the divine being as the person of the Father under the heading of subordinationism in *God in Patristic Thought* (Eugene, OR: Wipf & Stock, 2008), pp. 132–33, 142–45, 254. Even in this scheme, the Son is to be distinguished from the creaturely order in that He participates in the divine being by nature and not by grace. Ibid., pp. 142–43.

In spite of the limitation of existing theologies of divine being examined in preceding segments, they do not err in describing non-ontological but nevertheless important aspects of God's being. At any rate, their two most significant contributions are negative and developmental: the clear failure to address the ontological oneness of God by preferring instead qualitative or relational conceptions of the same, which highlights the importance of the matter, and the bequeathing of the concept of interdependence within the divine being.

The total effect of available conceptions of the being of God is the furnishing of categories on the basis of which one must arrive at an articulation of the divine substance. Existing theologies, positively and negatively, proffer ontological and relational interdependence as crucial categories by which to understand the being of God through His triple personhood.

The Cappadocian Fathers and Augustine conceive of the divine reality as three ontologically independent divine persons with the same makeup, will, purpose, and action, leading to an understanding of the divine being as individual makeup, orientation and action, making for a oneness of substance, will, and action.

Both modifying and adding to that conception are theologians like J. D. Zizioulas, C. E. Gunton, and T. A. Smail, who conceptualize the divine reality as three ontologically independent but relationally interdependent divine persons with the same makeup, will, purpose, and action, so that the divine being is understood as relational dynamic, possessing a oneness of the principle of wellbeing, of shared life and community. A key representative of this kind of thinking, Zizioulas has directly equated the divine being with the communion of three persons that is the Trinity.[7]

A Possible Solution: *Perichoretic Constitution*

To do justice to the scriptural affirmation of the oneness of God as ontological, of the name of God as referring to a single personal being rather than functioning impersonally as the collective name of a group of entities, or as the name of an abstraction, it may be necessary to think of the divine reality as three ontologically and relationally interde-

---

[7] J. D. Zizioulas, 'On Being a Person: Towards an Ontology of Personhood', in *Persons, Divine and Human: King's College Essays in Theological Anthropology*, ed. C. Schwöbel and C. E. Gunton (Edinburgh: T&T Clark, 1991), p. 40. See also idem., 'The Doctrine of the Holy Trinity: The Significance of the Cappadocian Contribution', in *Trinitarian Theology Today: Essays on Divine Being and Act*, ed. C. Schwöbel and C. E. Gunton (Edinburgh: T&T Clark, 1995), p. 58.

pendent divine persons with the same makeup, will, purpose, and action, to conceive of the divine being[8] as divine consciousness in proto-divine person mutually constituted makeup and orientation so as recognize a oneness of a mutually constituted ontological principle.[9]

Such a conception of the divine being draws on the idea of a mutual indwelling and interpenetration given to the Greek term περιχώρησις and applied to the divine persons.[10] George Prestige observes that the doctrine is a logical implication of the concept of the divine substance being possessed fully, individually, this understood quantitatively as well as qualitatively, and shared equally by the three divine persons.[11]

This study proposes that it is helpful to apply the concept of περιχώρησις to the ontological interdependence[12] of the divine persons to create an idea of a *perichoretic constitution* in which the concept of personhood is *ontologized* and the concept of being or substance is *personalized*.[13] The divine reality is to be understood in terms of an ontologi-

---

[8] And, for that matter, the divine person.

[9] In this way, sense can be made of scripture which apparently equates the Son and the Holy Spirit; namely, 2 Cor. 3:18, highlighted by Thomas Smail in *Reflected Glory: The Spirit in Christ and Christians* (London: Hodder and Stoughton, 1977), pp. 24–25.

[10] See V. Lossky, *The Mystical Theology of the Eastern Church* (Crestwood, NY: St. Vladimir's Seminary Press, 1976), pp. 53–54; G. Bray, *The Doctrine of God*, Contours of Christian Theology (Downers Grove, IL: InterVarsity Press, 1993), p. 158; R. Letham, *The Holy Trinity: In Scripture, History, Theology, and Worship* (Phillipsburg, NJ: P&R, 2004), p. 178.

[11] Prestige, *God in Patristic Thought*, pp. 284, 289.

[12] The idea of an ontological dependence within the Trinity may have existed since the patristic age, to which Augustine of Hippo bears witness in *Trin.* 6.1–3; either that, or Augustine misread the theology of defenders of orthodoxy like Athanasius of Alexandria, who appears to be one of the persons to whom Augustine refers seeing that he specifies individuals engaged in the fight against Arianism, and Athanasius writes of the things which Augustine cites, in *C. Ar.* 1.14 (Newman and Robertson, *NPNF*[2] 4:314–15). It is unnecessary to suppose that in holding to a view of the Son as the wisdom of the Father, Athanasius is thereby contradicting the doctrine of the equal divinity of the Father, Son, and Holy Spirit. This is because the Son may be perceived as being the wisdom of the Father in the same way that He is the Son of the Father; that is to say, in the sense of a role freely chosen in eternity, in which case 'Wisdom' as referring to the Son becomes a title. For an explanation of why the divine hierarchy does not imply ontological difference, see the earlier discussion of the theology of the divine being of Gregory Nyssen. Even if the concept of ontological dependence within the Trinity did exist during patristic times, it is to be distinguished from the idea of an ontological *inter*dependence within the divine being.

[13] In this way, the condition for a mutual containment is met: that the containing entity comprises the inherent part of the entity contained. It is to be noted that the idea of a mutual containment is firmly scriptural, witnessed to by John 17:21b-d.

cal, internal interdependence, an ontological περιχώρησις, and the divine persons as ontologically overlapping entities with a common being.[14]

In this way, there is only one being but three centers of consciousness, each of which is free to control that being however he desires without that use being limited in any way by that of the other two centers of consciousness. By virtue of their common being, these three centers of consciousness always agree and act in exactly the same ways, their effort always resulting in only one, unified action. When God is spoken of as one, either the Father, or the Son, or the Holy Spirit is spoken of, because the Father is the one God, the Son is the one God, and the Holy Spirit is the one God.

God does not exist in an abstract, impersonal form but in three personal forms. Therefore, when the Trinity is spoken of, in effect, the one God is being spoken of three times over. The only difference consists in the following: the Father is the one God with the identity of the Father;[15] the Son is the one God with the identity of the Son; and the Holy Spirit is the one God with the identity of the Holy Spirit. It may also be said that the one God is the Father, in whom are the Son and Holy Spirit; or the one God is the Son, in whom are the Father and the Holy Spirit; or the one God is the Holy Spirit, in whom are the Father and the Son.[16]

---

[14] Coffey's grasp of the concept of personhood lends itself to the idea of a common being in *Deus Trinitas*, p. 82; the present proposal was also partly inspired by Augustine's psychological analogy of the memory, intelligence, and will. John Feinberg in *No One Like Him: The Doctrine of God*, Foundations of Evangelical Theology (Wheaton, IL: Crossway Books, 2001), p. 484, reads the Cappadocian Fathers as maintaining a view of the Father, Son, and Holy Spirit as sharing in an essence that is numerically one. This interpretation, which according to David Brown in *The Divine Trinity* (La Salle, IL: Open Court, 1985), pp. 240–41, 289–93, belongs also to J. N. D. Kelly, contrasts with the interpretation of the Cappadocians as set forth in this paper, and which is that of Brown himself, and constitutes a misunderstanding in which a qualitative element (being) is conflated with a quantitative (number of entities) one. Be that as it may, Feinberg's perspective of a common divine being coheres with the present proposal. The writer records his gratitude to D. R.-S. Lang for suggesting the term 'common being' in place of an original 'shared being', which might imply that the divine being is partitioned out to the three divine persons rather than each having the fullness of the divine being.

[15] By which one is able to make sense of what is said about the Father being the only immortal entity in 1. Tim. 6:16.

[16] In this way, Stanley Grenz's crucial observation concerning the Old Testament presentation of God as a single person is addressed. J. S. Sexton, 'Conclusion', in *Two Views on the Doctrine of the Trinity*, ed. J. S. Sexton and S. N. Gundry, Counterpoints (Grand Rapids, MI: Zondervan, 2014), p. 214. Karl Barth, too, speaks of God as a single person. P. M. Collins, *Trinitarian Theology: West and East: Karl Barth, the Cappadocian Fathers, and John Zizioulas* (Oxford: Oxford University Press, 2001), p. 175. Furthermore, the concept of the Trinity here is in keeping with Kathryn Tanner's insight in *Jesus, Humanity and the Trinity*, pp. 38–39.

This does not therefore mean that there are three Gods. To say that there are three Gods is to say that there are three divine entities each with his own, unique being. In the foregoing formulation, however, the Father, the Son, and the Holy Spirit are conceived as three entities but with one, common being.[17] To the question of whether there is one God, tantamount to asking if there is one divine entity with his own, unique being, one must answer in the affirmative: the Father is such an entity; the Son, too, is such an entity; and the Holy Spirit, as well, is such an entity.

Yet there is no implication here of there being three Gods, or three independent subjects. This is because in order to obtain the result of three Gods, one has to go from one to two and then from two to three. Nonetheless, it is not possible to take even the first step. The moment one tries to look for the one God among the Father, the Son, and the Holy Spirit, and, considering any one of them individually, finds him, the search cannot continue, since there is no more entity with his own, unique being to be identified. The other two divine persons cannot stand as candidates because their common being, and for that matter their respective centers of consciousness, have already been considered, leaving no other divine entity with his own, unique being to be counted as another God.

The writer would like to suggest that this theory does not violate the principle or raison d'être underlying Karl Barth's concept of a single divine subjectivity, which seems to be at least partly calculated to forestall the notion of there being three Gods rather than one.[18] This is for the reason that three Gods, as typically understood from pagan mythologies, do not necessarily act in exactly the same way. In fact, there may be disagreement within the pantheon. Nor are pagan gods imagined to possess precisely the same cognitive and conative disposition.

This state of affairs obviously does not obtain with the Father, the Son, and the Holy Spirit. The divine persons have an identical substance. This, in itself, is sufficient to counter the groundless accusation that they constitute three deities, as David Brown has adroitly demonstrated from the teaching of the Cappadocian Fathers. Yet, according to our proposal, the divine persons are not simply entities which are exactly like one another in every possible way but they are in possession of a numerically and absolutely identical being—one and the same.

---

[17] This agrees with Prestige's articulation of the Trinity in *God in Patristic Thought*, pp. 168, 177–78.

[18] D. O. Sumner, 'Obedience and Subordination in Karl Barth's Trinitarian Theology', in *Advancing Trinitarian Theology: Explorations in Constructive Dogmatics*, ed. O. D. Crisp and F. Sanders, Los Angeles Theology Conference (Grand Rapids, MI: Zondervan, 2014), 140–41.

There is an otherness in God that is real and that allows for fellowship between the divine persons. Concurrently, the planning, willing, and acting are acts of a single subject.[19] The two criteria can only be upheld on the premise that there are three cognitive and conative entities, completely and categorically identical with one another except in respect to their distinctive self-awareness, and self-identity. Notice that the divine persons have not been distinguished on the basis of individual existence, for they do not by themselves have the power of independent existence.

If the three persons did not possess cognitive and conative capacity, there could not be authentic fellowship between them unless the word were taken in an extremely metaphorical and wrong-headed sense to indicate close proximity of some mechanical, non-social kind. In addition, if the divine persons possessed anything less than a numerically identical being, they could not begin to be adverted to as a single subject. So, how might God be conceived as a single subject? This can be done through striking a distinction between God viewed externally and internally. Considered as a being, which effectively entails ignoring the threefold internal differentiation of the divine being, God is just one, whether the being considered is the Father, the Son, or the Holy Spirit.

On balance, the concept of a single divine subjectivity is not diametrically opposed to the notion of the divine persons as cognitive and conative centers of consciousness. The real issue, if there is any, with applying a modern concept of personhood to the divine being is a substantial rather than formal or dimensional one, a question not so much of whether the divine persons have *formally* distinct centers of consciousness, but whether these very centers are *substantially* distinct. As David Brown has highlighted, the form of personhood alone does not insure against the malady of tritheism;[20] in truth, it is really quite irrelevant to the discussion. What matters is that the persons as cognitive and conative centers of consciousness are formally distinct but substantially identical.

In sum, it is not erroneous to say that there are three ways in which the search for the one God can transpire: beginning and ending either with the Father, with the Son, or with the Holy Spirit. Consequently, the only way to fully encompass the divine reality with its multiple forms of self-awareness and self-identity grounded in one, common being, though not divine character and power which each of the persons has in fullness of perfection, is not to speak of the one God, but to speak of the Father, the Son, and the Holy Spirit.

---

[19] Ibid., p. 141.
[20] Brown, *Divine Trinity*, p. 296.

One is hard-pressed, like Augustine was, to identify suitable analogies for the Trinity. A reasonable illustration can be given using two examples: the first is of three people with the same mind, who think the same things, make the same decisions, do the same things, and who are always together, three persons who are so linked that whatever happens to one will also happen to the other two, because they have the same mind and same body though it may look as if they have three different minds and bodies; the second and better example is of an unbreakable dance[21] of three partners who are so deeply in love with each other that they do not ever wish to separate; the limitation, however, of this example is that it implies that the partners could choose to separate as has to happen with any dance, but this is not possible with the Trinity, for the moment one divine person is removed from the circle, if that were at all possible, all three would cease to be persons, to be divine, and God would cease, in a sense, to exist.[22]

It may be well to conclude with a scheme that describes the relationship between the divine persons in regard to their being. To account for the idea of an ontological interdependence within the godhead, it is necessary to postulate that each divine person, in bare essence logically but not temporally prior to mutual interpenetration, possesses a faculty unique to himself, so that it is only as the three persons come together that they each have full use of a personal faculty or the faculty that endows a self with the qualities of personhood.[23]

---

[21] The illustration and analogy of the dance in relation to the Trinity has previously been used by C. S. Lewis and Timothy Keller. C. S. Lewis, *Mere Christianity* (New York: Macmillan, 1977), p. 151 (cited in T. Keller, *King's Cross: The Story of the World in the Life of Jesus* [London: Hodder, 2013], pp. 4–8). See also T. Keller, *The Reason for God: Belief in an Age of Scepticism* (London: Hodder, 2009), pp. 214–15.

[22] Cf. Zizioulas' remarks in *Lectures in Christian Dogmatics* (London: T&T Clark, 2008), pp. 26 and 53.

[23] This is in keeping with Barth's concept, as presented by Eberhard Jüngel in *God's Being Is In Becoming: The Trinitarian Being of God in the Theology of Karl Barth. A Paraphrase*, trans. J. Webster (Grand Rapids, MI: William B. Eerdmans, 2001), pp. 42–45, of the Trinitarian being of God as occurring in a communion of the Father, Son, and Holy Spirit. Barth's seminal idea is that the relationship between the divine persons triggers and stimulates divine being. In this way he makes divine being dependent on the actions of the divine persons. The oneness of God, then, is contingent on the actions of the three divine persons who must and will hold themselves together in unity. The divine being is not fellowship alone but the Father, Son, and Holy Spirit *in* fellowship. In other words, it is a situation, or, to use a term Barth would prefer, an *event*. While in so asserting Barth becomes guilty of a radical redefinition of the divine being, he echoes the development of the present discussion by furnishing the concept of the divine being as a state to be entered into by the divine persons. See a comparable understanding in C. E. Gunton, *Becoming and Being: The Doctrine of God in Charles Hartshorne and Karl Barth*, 2nd ed. (London: SCM, 2001), pp. 138, 142–43, 148, 150. Pannenberg expresses a similar viewpoint to Barth. W. Pannenberg, 'Eternity, Time,

There is no suggestion here of any temporal progression in the internal being of God, or of a progressive evolution as it were of the internal features of the deity. No time needs to elapse for these actions described as taking place within the divine being nor do they occur in time. God does not need time to perform any intrinsic action, as he demonstrated in creating the world by his mere word. Moreover, God does not perform any intrinsic action at a particular point in time since the idea of a point in time presupposes earlier points in time so that it may legitimately be asked why God did not perform that intrinsic action earlier, an endless flow of time preceding that action. This is a logical impossibility, because of the implication that from one perspective, that of the endless past, God never began to perform that action. Perhaps in regard to God in His being it is better to think not in terms of time and change but eternal actualization.

Within the being of God, no potentiality exists;[24] every intrinsic action that God wills to be done and is capable of performing is completed. At no 'point' in 'time' were they unaccomplished. Nevertheless the effects of these intrinsic actions are real, even though it is impossible to locate their origin for there is none, as much as God is real, even though it is impossible to locate His origin for there is none. It may be preferable and more logically coherent to think of the described process as a scripturally informed and truthful way of depicting the mutual dependence of the divine persons by means of speculation and supposition about what would happen if a logically and conceptually possible but practically impossible situation obtained; this situation being the sundering of the communion of the divine persons, a tearing of the three one from another and an individualization of the persons.

This process, then, is best seen as a way of speaking about the internal and relational structure of the divine being, of the eternally actualized potentialities of its principle. As such, God's intrinsic actions have no real existence as actions but only in the form of their ultimate and final effects. With this in mind, discussion, as this section contains, of

---

and the Trinitarian God', in *Trinity, Time, and Church: A Response to the Theology of Robert W. Jenson*, ed. C. E. Gunton (Grand Rapids, MI: William B. Eerdmans, 2000), pp. 69–70. Also consult P. G. Heltzel and C. T. Collins Winn, 'Karl Barth, reconciliation, and the Triune God', in *The Cambridge Companion to The Trinity*, ed. P. C. Phan (Cambridge: Cambridge University Press, 2011), p. 179.

[24] R. T. Mullins, 'An Analytic Response to Stephen R. Holmes, with a Special Treatment of his Doctrine of Divine Simplicity', in *The Holy Trinity Revisited: Essays in Response to Stephen R. Holmes*, ed. T. A. Noble and J. S. Sexton, Christian Doctrines in Historical Perspective (Milton Keynes, England: Paternoster, 2015), p. 87. See also S. R. Holmes, 'Trinitarian Action and Inseparable Operations: Some Historical and Dogmatic Reflections', in *Advancing Trinitarian Theology: Explorations in Constructive Dogmatics*, ed. O. D. Crisp and F. Sanders, Los Angeles Theology Conference (Grand Rapids, MI: Zondervan, 2014), p. 70.

a proto-Father, proto-Son, and proto-Holy Spirit is merely theoretical. There never was a time when God existed in the forms of proto-divine persons. God has always existed and will always exist in the forms of the fully personal Father, the Son, and the Holy Spirit.

To return to the exposition of the scheme concerning the mutual interdependence within the divine being, one might postulate that the Father has wisdom as a unique principle, the Son, will or agency of decision-making, and the Holy Spirit, agency of action or execution and affect.[25] Let the bare essence, logically prior to mutual interpenetration, of each of the pre-personal entities, be defined thus: the proto-Father comprises a controlling center as well as the unique principle of wisdom; the proto-Son comprises a controlling center as well as the unique principle of will or agency of decision-making; the proto-Holy Spirit comprises a controlling center as well as the unique principle of agency of action or execution and affect.

Interpenetration of these three proto-persons is not simply logically possible but logically necessary. This is because the wisdom of the Father contains the unchangeable idea and plan of interpenetration and communion and all that it implies, including loving relationship with the other two persons, and creation of the world for relationship with creatures, and causes the proto-Father to initiate interpenetration with the proto-Son, who possesses the agency of decision-making, the will to follow through with his unchangeable idea and plan, altruistically, so as to endue the proto-Son with his wisdom. In

---

[25] This attribution is by no means arbitrary or speculative. It adheres to the threefold scheme of the divine operation of Gregory Nyssen whereby the Father is the possessor of the plans or the things to be done, the Son, the one who initiates its fulfillment, and the Spirit, the one who executes its fulfillment, as well as to that of Boethius, who speaks of a person as a conscious, cognitive and conative entity, according to J. Moltmann, *The Trinity and the Kingdom: The Doctrine of God*, trans. M. Kohl (Minneapolis, MN: Fortress Press, 1993), p. 171. Furthermore, the difference between the faculties inherent to each proto-person, which is of no ontological significance in regard to the full persons, adds justification to the assignment of the roles which the Father, the Son, and the Holy Spirit have mutually chosen to take up in that the superior role is given on the basis of respect and deference to he who is ontologically superior as a *proto-person*. This resolves an important complication created by the view of the divine hierarchy as constituted by roles freely chosen and assumed: whether the names of the Father, Son, and Holy Spirit have any essential meaning reflective of the nature of the entities which bear them. An affirmative answer can be given by means of a scheme in which the ontological superiority of the proto-persons, though not of the full persons, is propounded. For a further discussion of divine hierarchy, see the analysis of the concept of the divine being of Gregory Nyssen. As for the Holy Spirit being assigned the faculty of affect, this is predicated on the fact, as per Augustine of Hippo, that the Spirit is *vinculum amoris*, a "bond of love", between the Father and the Son, and the spirit, whether of God or a human being, is an integral part that is able to feel (cf. Dan. 7:15, Eph. 4:30, Rom. 8:26), and be affected by being blasphemed against, or lied to.

interpenetrating the proto-Son, the proto-Father is himself endowed with the agency of decision-making or will of the proto-Son.

Then, the proto-Father and proto-Son both initiate interpenetration with the proto-Holy Spirit, who possesses the agency of action or execution and affect, the last process required to bring about full personhood, out of a wish to endue the proto-Holy Spirit with their wisdom and agency of decision-making or will. In interpenetrating the proto-Holy Spirit, the proto-Father and proto-Son are themselves endowed with the agency of action or execution and affect.[26]

With the interpenetration of the three proto-persons, each becomes a full person in communion with the others.[27] Upon mutual consultation and confirmation concerning roles, the divine persons acquire the central identities of Father, Son, and Holy Spirit. Again, these events do not form a temporal but logical sequence.

In this scheme, the Father can be defined ontologically as comprising the controlling center of the Father and the principle which is unique to him; that is, wisdom; the controlling center of the Son and the principle which is unique to him; that is, will or the agency of decision-making; and the controlling center of the Holy Spirit and the principle which is unique to him; that is, the agency of action or execution and affect; all of which is headed and directed by the controlling center of the Father.

Likewise, the Son can be defined ontologically as comprising the controlling center of the Father and the principle which is unique to him; that is, wisdom; the controlling center of the Son and the principle which is unique to him; that is, will or the agency of decision-making; and the controlling center of the Holy Spirit and the principle which is

---

[26] Fitting the theological framework of Basil of Caesarea, as noted by Prestige, *God in Patristic Thought*, pp. 171–72.

[27] See the discussion in Prestige, *God in Patristic Thought*, pp. 291 and 295. The scheme proposed by this study is what would result from applying pseudo-Cyril of Alexandria's idea of the two natures of Christ to the three persons of the Trinity, conceived as ontologically interdependent. In the case of pseudo-Cyril, according to Prestige, however, the idea is of a common divine identity rather than a common divine being; it is where the divine persons do not conceive of themselves as separate entities but as one entity. Ibid., pp. 284, 295–301. Yet, if the divine persons do not think of themselves as separate entities, how is it that Jesus, the Son, could refer to the Father? In the estimation of this writer, as such, Prestige takes a wrong-headed approach to an understanding of the divine being in prioritizing etymology rather than anchoring his proposal on the question of the extent to which existing theological ideas of the divine being conform to the biblical witness. cf. Ibid., pp. 168–69, 301. Olson and Hall read the Cappadocians as espousing a similar idea. R. E. Olson and C. A. Hall, *The Trinity*, Guides to Theology (Grand Rapids, MI: William B. Eerdmans, 2002), p. 36. On a separate note, the scheme of this study does not violate the principle that each person should be defined by a unique relation, as hinted in Moltmann, *Trinity and the Kingdom*, p. 182.

unique to him; that is, the agency of action or execution and affect; all of which is headed and directed by the controlling centre of the Son.

Finally, the Holy Spirit can be defined ontologically as comprising the controlling center of the Father and the principle which is unique to him; that is, wisdom; the controlling center of the Son and the principle which is unique to him; that is, will or the agency of decision-making; and the controlling center of the Holy Spirit and the principle which is unique to him; that is, the agency of action or execution and affect; all of which is headed and directed by the controlling center of the Holy Spirit.[28]

The Father, the Son, and the Holy Spirit coexist eternally as three persons in one being. Their common personal faculty does not preclude their coexistence or limit the ability of each in any way; the first because the consciousnesses are ontological realities, as are their persons; and the second because the faculties of wisdom, will, and agency of action and affect are infinite in capacity.[29]

It may be queried whether even in an infinite personal faculty, the three persons occupy each only a third of the total. The response must be in the affirmative. At the same time, one is requested to remember that the divine persons perform their actions instantly. If this is the case, and if the divine persons regularly rotate their 'sections' of the common personal faculty such that each would have occupied every section of the entire faculty on the performance of three actions, and if this cycle of three actions takes no more time to complete than any one of those actions, one understands how each divine person is able to occupy the whole faculty, albeit across three actions, without preventing the other two from doing the same.

Even in a scenario where no action is performed, the same sequence holds, and the divine persons rotate sections of the common personal faculty so that each possesses the complete faculty across two instantaneous movements. In eternity, where no action is possible, and all potentiality is achieved, the three divine persons nonetheless exist in continuous rotation so as to each possess his fullness of being. Accordingly, the divine being exists in eternal dynamic. To the extent that it is impossible to separate the divine persons one from another, it is impossible to consider the divine being except in a cycle of three movements in which each divine person possesses the fullness of being. Likewise, insomuch as the divine beings have never existed without full personhood apart

---

[28] This is in harmony with Boethius' view as cited in Moltmann, *Trinity and the Kingdom*, p. 171.

[29] To say of the proto-persons that they possess unique principles of full personhood is not to imply that the other persons do not have these attributes in the smallest measure; they do.

from one another, the same have never not existed in a cycle of three movements, having a 'rotational' nature of existence.[30]

In this way, the one God is able to relate with the one God, even though the being of God is only numerically one.[31] A superficial way of summarizing the theory of *perichoretic constitution* is that the divine persons contain one another in the sense of making up one another.

Biblical Basis

Far from empty speculation, the theory presented above is really based on the strong intimations of Scripture. Prov. 8:22 was brought to the center of controversy when the followers of the presbyter Arius alleged that the word קָנָה, which is to be rendered with the meaning of 'to make', proves the ontological inferiority of the Son of God, who Scripture apparently says was made by the Father.[32] This translation need not be disputed. Indeed, it serves as evidence of the biblical origin and basis of the divine ontological scheme previously propounded. Michael Fox explains why ownership is not a possible signification, only making or taking into ownership.[33] In this instance, making and taking into ownership are ideas that fit the theological scheme perfectly.

The identification of the figure of wisdom in the Hebrew Bible with the second person of the Trinity has been suggested at least from the time of Origen.[34] Viewing the

---

[30] This cycle is to be regarded as a movement of being rather than an action, which is not permitted in eternity. If it is asked how movement such as this could exist in timeless eternity, it may be riposted that it is just as reasonable as accepting that particular attributes are essential to God. To the possible question of whether the divine being is thereby bound by nature to be what he has not willed to become so that the freedom of God is undermined, the response is that the divine being as divine person wills or wishes to be what he is, as Turcescu has underscored in Nyssen's theology of divine personhood in *Gregory of Nyssa and the Concept of Divine Persons*, p. 5. Furthermore, it is to be clarified that the divine being cannot make a choice to be what he is that is prior to his being what he is in light of the facts that he has never been other than what he is, and that he *is* what he is, as per the doctrine of divine simplicity, so that the issue of God not being capable of willing to be what he is antecedent to being what he is, is a wrongheaded one, at least in this scheme.

[31] Sumner, 'Obedience and Subordination', pp. 140–41.

[32] Athanasius of Alexandria, *C. Ar.* 1.53 (Newman and Robertson, *NPNF*² 4:337); and idem., *C. Ar.* 2.18 (Newman and Robertson, *NPNF*² 4:357–58).

[33] M. V. Fox, *Proverbs 1—9*, AB 18A (New Haven, CT: Yale University Press, 2000), p. 279.

[34] Prestige, *God in Patristic Thought*, p. 175.

passage backwards through the lenses of the ontological proposal, one sees that the 'making' of wisdom by the Lord, the Father, is to be linked with the way in which, in the internal structure of the divine being, the proto-Father in communing with the proto-Son, in the former's perichoretic 'entering into' the latter, makes His wisdom accessible to the latter, in effect making a new entity defined by the wisdom of the proto-Father so that it is not incorrect to say that the proto-Father 'made' wisdom; that is, the proto-Son as availing of the wisdom of the proto-Father.

How then might it be said that the Lord, the Father in the fullness of His personhood, made the Son as wisdom in the fullness of His personhood as though He engaged in some such work at a particular point in time? Let it be remembered first that the proto-divine persons are not ontological realities but theoretical constructs which do not lend themselves easily to specific reference in what appears to be a simple account of the internal structure of the divine being where complete metaphysical precision is not entailed. Second, to speak of the Father as having made the Son as wisdom in the inception of his work as in the English Standard Version does not amount to an assertion that such an act took place in time. Rather, pace Fox, the statement is to be comprehended as referring to a state that obtained even before anything was created; prior to God's creation of the world, the Son was already 'made' as wisdom by the Father in the eternal interpenetration of Father and Son, a state of affairs that has never not existed and will always exist, for that is the only way God can exist.

The Scripture also accounts elegantly for the other translation of קָנָה; namely, as 'took into ownership'. As the proto-Father enters into the proto-Son and endows him with the former's wisdom, the proto-Son necessarily enters into the proto-Father, in so doing giving the proto-Father access to the will of the proto-Son. In their interpenetration, the proto-Father takes into ownership all that the proto-Son is, just as the proto-Son takes into ownership all that the proto-Father is.

Once again, the Scripture's depiction of the Father as taking the Son into ownership is not to be looked to for exact metaphysical accuracy, nor does it comprise a witness to some act that took place at some point in time. Instead, the reader is to understand in the passage a crucial note of the fact that before the creation of the world the Son was already taken into ownership by the Father in the eternal interpenetration of the Father and the Son, a state of affairs that has never not existed and will always exist, for that is the only way God can exist.

A similar signification is contained in the word נִסַּ֫כְתִּי in Prov. 8:23, translated in the ESV with the meaning of erection, but with another more possible rendering of being pieced together like a garment or constituted, the second of which comports better with the meaning of קָנָה as 'to make'[35] but, in light of the scheme, both are equally likely and perhaps complementary.

No less importantly, Prov. 8 bears testimony to the commitment to their respective roles of the Father, Son, and Holy Spirit upon their mutual constitution. Scripture does this through the use of the term חִיל, which has been rendered with the meaning of 'to make a son'.[36] Once more, this is not to be taken as a reference to an act of begetting that occurred in time, but as pointing to an eternal state of affairs that prevailed even prior to the creation of the world (Prov. 8:24–25).

While there is no explicit scriptural evidence touching in a similar fashion on the internal constitutive relationship between the Holy Spirit and the Father and the Son, the writer takes his lead from the biblical affirmation that the three divine persons are of equal ontological status, and thereby suggests the Holy Spirit as also inherently a proto-person with a principle required by all the divine persons, receiving from and giving to the proto-Father and the proto-Son just as the proto-Son received from and gave to the proto-Father.

Doctrinal Basis

Insofar as Christ is the second person of the Trinity, and Rahner's rule[37] holds true, any theory concerning the immanent Trinity must tell of how the incarnation has affected internal Trinitarian relations if at all. The relationship, however, is bilateral, since there is nothing stopping a theologian from forming a theory of the incarnation prior to dealing with the Trinity. Both approaches are equally valid. For the purpose of identifying a doctrinal basis for the theory of the immanent Trinity proposed above, however, it is necessary to work our way from the incarnation toward the Trinity, and to see what justification we may find in the account of the earthly life and ministry of the Lord Jesus that

---

[35] Fox, *Proverbs 1—9*, p. 281.
[36] Which, Fox notes, most probably signifies birth. Ibid., p. 282.
[37] See K. Rahner, *The Trinity*, trans. J. Donceel (New York: Crossroad, 1997).

would facilitate general acceptance of our Trinitarian proposition of a *perichoretic constitution*.

The observation regarding Christ's dependence on the Father and the Holy Spirit is commonplace. Even the nature of that reliance has been noted: Christ's teachings and deeds originate from the Father.[38] By considering the extent to which Christ has to lean on the Father for his speech and action, one may arrive at an understanding of his powers whilst still in the earthly phase of his life. If it is supposed that the reliance were categorical and absolute, as Scripture appears to suggest,[39] the apparent implication would have to be that Christ voluntarily made himself for all intents and purposes no more powerful or capable than any other human being.

Readers of the Gospels realize that Christ's life was characterized by an insuperable desire to carry out the will of the Father in heaven which is his. No impression is given to the effect that Christ ever sought to fulfill a desire which was his alone and not also the Father's. In very fact, the concept of the 'time' upon which Christ waited to act on the will of the Father infers that the Lord did not merely act on his Father's instructions, speaking the words and doing the deeds he was commanded to, but that he also did all these in accordance to the schedule of the Father.

In the most absolute sense of the word, Christ's earthly existence was scripted from beginning to end. This is not to say that among all entities only Christ's existence was fully predestined by God; there is no doubt that the sovereignty of God encompasses every created thing. The point of significance here is that Christ was fully aware of his schedule, and adhered to it in an uncompromising way, even up to Calvary.[40]

That this is redolent of the manner in which, according to our theory of the immanent Trinity, the divine persons of the Son and the Holy Spirit equally depend on the wisdom or plan that as per the internal relational structure of the divine being is the unique principle of the proto-Father is unmistakable. In a very real sense, the wisdom of the Son and the Holy Spirit is the wisdom of the Father, since the proto-Father does not actually exist. Here, then, is evidence from no other source than scripture that may be adduced in support of the theory of *perichoretic constitution* on the basis of the way in which it is reflected in intra-Trinitarian relations.

---

[38] See, for example, J. I. Packer, *Knowing God* (London: Hodder & Stoughton, 2004), pp. 67–69. Also see Keller, *King's Cross*, p. 6.

[39] See, for instance, John 5:19, 30; 7:16; 8:28; 12:49–50.

[40] E.g. Luke 9:51 and Mark 10:32.

Granted that the Gospels may be interpreted to substantiate the view of the Son as carrying out the will of the Father, and thereby being dependent on his wisdom, how is the role of the Holy Spirit fleshed out in the narrative? The third person of the Trinity is frequently mentioned in connection with the idea of power;[41] that is, the effective outworking of the purposes of God in the realm of the created order. Might this not be testimony to the fact that Christ was able to bring the will of the Father to fruition only by means of the agency of the Holy Spirit indwelling him? Indeed, the very fact that Christ has to be replaced by the Holy Spirit as the helper and source of power for believers seems to indicate that the will of the Father which Christ came to earth to do could not be accomplished apart from the active participation and completing work of the Holy Spirit.

Is there any support for the view of Christ as the second person of the Trinity as comprehended by our doctrine? Christ is depicted in the Gospels as a determined agent of God. He does not vacillate even at the horrifying and looming prospect of crucifixion. It has been claimed that the prayers of Christ during his last moments prior to execution in the garden of Gethsemane illustrate his human struggle to obey the will of God. This line of interpretation need not be the only option exegetically available. Indeed, if there was a part of Christ which hesitated to perform the decree of the Father, he would have manifested that indecisiveness in some wise, but this did not occur at Gethsemane. Instead, Christ showed himself to be at all points in submission to God.

Yes, he did say to the Father requesting for his lot to be removed from his hand if it could. Yet, these are not the words of an indecisive person. They express the pain of someone who *knows* and has come to full *acceptance* of his calling and mission, but who at a crucial point is suddenly overcome by emotion so that he pleads for something[42] that in his more rational moments he knows is impossible yet soon after regains his composure.[43] These trenchant words of Christ constitute a controlled outpouring of feeling in the face of unimaginable humiliation and pain, and of death.

This reading is confirmed by that which follows immediately after; the expression of his desire for God's will to prevail. Here is a man who knows full well that the only possible outcome is not that a cruel death might be deferred or even averted by heartfelt pleading. In consequence, though he was abruptly overwhelmed by fear of death and the

---

[41] E.g. Luke 4:14.

[42] Namely, for the Passion to be delayed.

[43] Emotional breakdown is implied by F. Bovon, *Luke 3: A Commentary on the Gospel of Luke 19:28—24:53*, trans. J. Crouch, Hermeneia (Minneapolis, MN: Fortress, 2012), p. 201.

experience of abandonment by his Father, it was not so as to cause him to rebel against God. At all points he had subjected himself to the will of the Father, so that even in his deepest psychological distress he attached to an irrational request for deliverance words seeking the approval of God, for the idea of departing from the command of the Father was utterly repugnant to his nature.

If it continues to be disputed that Christ did not waver at Gethsemane, consider then the words of the Evangelist who recorded Christ as reminding his disciples in a stern rebuke that he was never in a state of mere acquiescence or resignation to the will of a domineering Father as it were, but he was only carrying out his own pleasure, which was to do the pleasure of his Father, to which he referred as his food.[44] He did this when he implied that if he did not want to surrender his life at the cross, all he had to do was call upon heaven and legions of angels would come to his aid and deliver him from his enemies.[45] Nonetheless, the will of the Father was the most important thing in his life, simply because it was his supreme delight.

This is obedience at its highest and best; this, manifestly, is the unique principle of the proto-Son according to the internal relational structure of the divine being: the will, and resolution to perform to the fullest and utmost the decree of the Father.

In these ways it may and must be asserted that the theory we have outlined above is fully in keeping with and reflective of the biblical record of the life and ministry of the Lord Jesus. By laying a doctrinal foundation for our proposition, we have felicitously also substantiated a position with which we began on the extent to which Christ depended on the Father and the Holy Spirit. Our answer must be that he depended fully and absolutely on them, as the Son in eternity depends fully and absolutely on the Father and the Holy Spirit.

The most crucial doctrinal implication of our theory, that there is no qualitative and substantial distinction between the human and divine natures, wills, and souls of Christ, that in fact the only distinction is an aspectual one, to be viewed using the categories of Christ's active (human), dormant (divine), and total (human and divine) existence, will be explored in the relevant section below. Another important result of our theory for Christology as it relates to the immanent Trinity is that the dependence of the human Christ on the Father and the Holy Spirit is by no means a feature only of his earthly life and ministry but, as a matter of fact, a reflection of the ontological interdependence of the divine persons from eternity. It is theologically significant that our proposition is de-

---

[44] John 4:34.
[45] Matt. 26:53.

monstrably rooted in scripture and doctrine, and not mere speculation, for all doctrine must appeal to these two sources for its assertions.

An Important Objection Refuted

This is the place to anticipate a potential objection that has been raised in another setting to an aspect of a certain theory of the immanent Trinity and due to the likeness between that theory and ours, may very well also be levelled against the latter. This has to do with whether the Son was indeed begotten, and the Holy Spirit, spirated, in eternity, prior to the act and event of creation.

The relevant discussion appears in a footnote in an essay by Keith Yandell.[46] John Feinberg mounts an exegetical argument, to which Yandell refers and directs the reader's attention, in rejection of the doctrines of the eternal generation of the Son and the eternal procession of the Holy Spirit, mooting that these ideas could be restricted to the understanding of their respective historical analogues, as Yandell has suggested in the previous citation. Feinberg prefers to remain agnostic in regard to internal distinctions within the immanent Trinity.[47]

Is there a compelling basis for jettisoning the doctrines of the eternal generation and procession? Perhaps it is better to ask if there is good reason to retain them. In the estimation of Feinberg, the doctrines are troublesome because on a literal level, they cannot be properly grasped.[48]

Due to the fact that the doctrines of the eternal generation of the Son and eternal procession of the Spirit cannot be comprehended in a direct and straightforward manner, a metaphorical reading and interpretation has been advocated whereby the various descriptions of the process of begetting and spirating are to be seen purely as pointers or representations of the relationships that obtain between the divine persons. Expressing therefore, for instance, that the Father transmits the divine essence to the Son is meant exclusively to evoke the notion of the paternal-filial relationship between the Father and

---

[46] K. Yandell, 'How Many Times Does Three Go Into One?' in *Philosophical and Theological Essays on the Trinity*, ed. T. McCall and M. C. Rea (Oxford: Oxford University Press, 2009), 157–58, n. 8.

[47] Feinberg, *No One Like Him*, pp. 487–92, citation from p. 492.

[48] Ibid., p. 489.

the Son into which they have eternally entered, without in any way implying that an ontological transference of matter had taken place between the two.

This is not dissimilar to the way in which people sometimes speak of someone as having been 'reborn' upon experiencing and overcoming a traumatic personal crisis. In this example, the idea of birth functions as a symbol to create an association between the dramatic change, that is, from non-existence to existence, that birth represents, and that the surmounting of personal trauma involves. The reference is purged of its literal meaning in order to point to a different but not utterly dissimilar referent. Such symbolism evidently has its uses. To be sure, gross misunderstanding may lead to a failure of that function,[49] yet this can be effectively eliminated by the placement of descriptions of the eternal generation and procession in the context of the doctrine of the attributes of God. Seen in that light, the doctrines serve to illuminate rather than obscure.

In point of fact, the doctrines secure the vital truths of the qualitative identity of the substance of the divine persons and its distinctiveness from that of any thing in the created order, as has already been noted. It may be recalled that St. Athanasius himself appealed to the divine relations of origin in averring the equality of the essence of the Son with the Father, who is acknowledged to be God.[50] In the face of such utility, a proposal to dispense with notions of eternal generation and procession of the Son and Spirit respectively must do more than show that these doctrines are not the only reasonable or possible interpretations of the scriptures on which they are typically grounded.

As a particularly important case in point, Feinberg has not demonstrated beyond all doubt that it is impossible for the declaration of God in Ps. 2:7 concerning his relationship with the Son to be an affirmation of the eternal generation of the second person of the Trinity. More significantly, the doctrines bequeath to the church a way of articulating the otherwise categorically ineffable relationship between the divine persons.

It must also be stated that the deployment of human procreative categories to communicate the self-identities and functions of the Father, the Son, and the Holy Spirit is intended to achieve a repentance from a humanism that is powerless to think in any other terms than its own. To speak of the Son as being eternally begotten is not to accept a diminution of the notion of begetting as it is normally understood in the human realm but a sublimation of the same to a higher and more proper sense. In any parent-child relationship, the core element and the matter that demands attention is not the fact

---

[49] This seems to be Feinberg's primary concern.
[50] Athanasius of Alexandria, *C. Ar.* 2.34 (Newman and Robertson, *NPNF²* 4:366) and idem., *C. Ar.* 3.4 (Newman and Robertson, *NPNF²* 4:395).

of the birth, essential as this is to the relationship, but the intimacy and quality of that relationship.[51]

The act or event of begetting is therefore not simply an act or event, but the portal to a greater reality; begetting represents in itself entrance into a new relationship. There is no need to introduce any real separation between the two things. For this reason, it is right and felicitous to the utmost for the concept of begetting or spirating to assume the meaning of the relationships, the one paternal-filial, and the other subjective-spiritual, to which they point as their sole signification in the case of the Trinity.

Finally, employment of procreative terms vis-à-vis relationship between the divine persons is aimed at preserving and underscoring the fact that the divine persons have their relationships with each other not by necessity, as is the case with human persons, who exist in familial relationships not because they have chosen that state of affairs but because they have been placed in them by the Creator, but only because the divine persons have chosen, eternally, to enter into those relationships as a parent chooses in most cases to have children. In a word, there has never been a time or a moment when any one of the three divine persons ever felt any less than completely pleased with the self-identities and functions they each distinctively possess.[52]

Beyond the reasons already canvassed, the argument against the doctrine of the eternal generation of the Son as articulated by John Feinberg is not exegetically insuperable, much as he might give that impression. If a passage like Ps. 2:7 afforded the strongest scriptural basis for the idea of an eternal generation of the Son, there might be cause for doing away with the belief. Yet, for all the comprehensiveness and adroitness of his argumentation, Feinberg has not satisfactorily addressed a key passage used to anchor the doctrine; namely, Prov. 8:24–25, previously cited, which makes reference to the begetting of the Son cast in the figure of Wisdom.

It might be demurred that the passage just mentioned does not necessarily anchor the idea of an eternal generation but merely one that is pre-historical in the sense of occurring antecedent to the creation of the world. To this it can be said in reply that there are just two 'moments' of 'begetting', so to speak, in the life of the Son; eternity, by which the Son 'becomes' and remains the Son, and the incarnation. If the incarnation is excluded as a 'time' of 'occurrence' by the fact that the 'event' of begetting mentioned in Prov. 8:24–25 transpired before the creation of the world, the only possibility left is the

---

[51] Similar to this is the differentiation some may make between a wedding, which is a one-time event, and a marriage, which is the relationship between spouses.

[52] Turcescu, *Gregory of Nyssa and the Concept of Divine Persons*, p. 5.

eternity of the divine being, making the reference by the passage to an eternal generation a logical and theological inevitability. While the objection might be raised to the effect that this line of reasoning is contingent on the assumption of the fact of the eternal generation, and thereby tautological, it should be noted that quite apart from any prior concept of an eternal generation, that the passage in Proverbs 8 points to that idea is a conclusion that can be logically deduced from the names of the divine persons.[53]

---

[53] The very names of the Father and the Son suggest that these eternal entities have an eternal paternal-filial relationship with each other.

Chapter 8

Implications:
Scriptural, Doctrinal, Ethical, Missional, and Practical

Scriptural Implications

The object of this section is to relate the result of the study to Scripture and to discuss how new light might be shed on its understanding. One of the manifest hermeneutical applications has to do with the hackneyed observation that the doctrine of the Trinity is nowhere to be found in the Hebrew Bible, which gives expression to faith in a single personal God as opposed to one existing in three divine persons. This, of course, is easily recognizable as a key objection and contention of Judaism. In a very different circle, painstaking effort is invested into unearthing witnesses to the triune nature of God in the form of divine manifestations sometimes regarded as the appearance of the second person of the Trinity, sometimes, of all three persons.

With the recovery of the concept of God as a single personal being via the idea of the three divine persons as possessing a numerically identical being, a third approach is made possible whereby testimony to God as single does not only do no harm to the Trinitarian doctrinal enterprise but really demands it. This is because the existence of the Father presupposes that of the Son and the Holy Spirit, is built upon them.[1] Apart from the giving, in the relational structure of the Godhead, of the proto-Father to the proto-

---

[1] Cf. J. D. Zizioulas, 'On Being a Person: Towards an Ontology of Personhood', in *Persons, Divine and Human: King's College Essays in Theological Anthropology*, ed. C. Schwöbel and C. E. Gunton (Edinburgh: T&T Clark, 1991), p. 41.

Son, who receives the gift of wisdom, and the giving of the proto-Son to the proto-Father, who receives the gift of the will, and the giving of the proto-Father and the proto-Son to the proto-Holy Spirit, who receives the gifts of wisdom and the will, and the giving of the proto-Holy Spirit to the proto-Father and the proto-Son, who receive the gift of agency of action, there is no possibility of a divine being.

To employ a simple analogy, the divine persons are like the sides of a triangle which is constantly subject to external pressure and in danger of imploding. Were any side to be lacking, the other two would quickly be pushed toward one another, and the shape would be lost. Only if the three sides are present can the triangular form be maintained. This form is the common personal faculty of the divine persons. It is thereby unwise to infer from a seeming dearth in the Old Testament of passages referring to three divine persons that there is no support for a Trinitarian doctrine. Wherever mention is made of 'God' or 'Lord', the Trinity is adverted to.

As a matter of fact, the numerical equivalence of the being of the three divine persons accords with an emphasis on God as a single personal being. It would be unusual, and needless, at least in the context of the Old Testament, for such inseparable divine persons to distinguish themselves clearly from one another.

The scheme of the divine being postulated in this study also enables alternative solutions to scriptural difficulties to be discovered. As a case in point, the ontology helps explain passages in which God is portrayed as speaking as if to himself.[2] Such scriptures offer insight into the inner life of God. It is here submitted that God was not speaking to himself, but that the Father was speaking to the Son and to the Holy Spirit, out of regard for them considering that they always act together. These two other persons are not named because they are already within, and indeed in their proto-forms co-compose with his, the being of the Father. So intertwined are the three divine persons that it is unnecessary for any one of them to do any more than speak in order to address the other two. This is a uniquely divine phenomenon.

As to why the biblical writer did not see a need to record explicitly that the Father was speaking specifically to the Son and to the Holy Spirit, this may well be because the purposes of the passages in question were not to detail the metaphysics of the being of God but to highlight the rationality behind his decisions.

The elegant complexity of the divine being can alone account for the divine testimony to Manoah,[3] regarding the sublime wonderment of the being of God. No proposal

---

[2] E.g. Gen. 6:7, 18:17–19.
[3] Judg. 13:18.

about the divine being is arrived at frivolously or without great effort. Always, the immense philosophical tools available to humankind are utilized in the service of theology proper. In the end, an intellectually satisfying and biblically faithful resolution to the logical dilemma of the Trinity does not constitute removal of the mystery that characterizes this doctrine, but a validation of the marvelousness of the being to which this doctrine points. To return to the immediate concern, it may well have been the case Manoah was not yet ready for a more complete exposition of the being of God, which would begin with the incarnation and first advent of the Son of God as the fully human and fully divine Jesus Christ.

Viewing God through the grid of the proposed ontology also 'humanizes' the deity somewhat in that no longer need God be seen as acting purely out of personal or even private emotion. When the Father acts, it is out of concern for the feelings of the Son. Consider the scene of the baptism of Jesus. When the newly baptized Son of God arose from the waters of the Jordan, the Father proclaimed that Jesus was his son, the object of his sheer delight. Here the Father was not merely expressing a private feeling which has little if anything to do with another, but he was really affirming his son.

In a similar way, whenever God in the Old Testament is reported to articulate some feeling of pain, anger, or even disgust, this does not have to be taken as evidence that God is simply self-absorbed; instead, it might be perceived as an exemplary instance of the Father being grieved or angered or disgusted not just because of the injustice he suffers but also and more importantly because the actions of the disobedient and wicked have grieved, angered, and disgusted the Son and the Holy Spirit, and the Father is communicating empathy as much as articulating his own feelings.[4]

Doctrinal Implications

Some of the clearest doctrinal implications of our theory of the immanent Trinity can be located in the area of Christology. The issue of the manner in which the divine and human in Christ relate one to the other deserves particular attention. The crucial and relevant insight from the understanding, inspired by the designation of unique principles in our proposition, of the relation between the will of Christ and that of his Father in his earthly life and ministry is that there is in terms of properties qualitatively common to

---

[4] This opens a new vista for thinking about the Pauline exhortation to share joy and sorrow in Rom. 12:15 as, perhaps, one involving an imitation of God.

both no substantial or qualitative distinction between the human and divine dimensions as they coexist in the single person of Christ.

The claim being made is that in Christ, in whom the fullness of the deity subsists, the human merely constitutes on the one hand a circumscription of the properties of the infinite divine being and on the other, the addition of a material human body with all its needs. These two things are interrelated, for the circumscription of the properties of the divine being transpires within the limits of the finite capacities of the human body, and in accordance to their natural growth and development.

This is why scripture relates that Christ grew in wisdom and stature as he matured as a child.[5] He always possessed the same properties in the same quantity and to the same degree as the Father and the Holy Spirit, even as a human being, and there being no substantial and qualitative difference between the human and divine with regard to properties qualitatively common to both, as much as the human capacity at its stage in development was able to contain, the non-moral properties were expressed and manifested, but since the properties of the divine being are infinite in degree, the fullness of them is not and cannot be expressed in the finite human body of Christ but hidden and concealed within the divine being, which is situated beneath the human nature of Christ.

Thus, in the human body, the properties of the Son of God like omnipresence, omniscience, and omnipotence were infinitely curtailed and made limited so that instead of being everywhere Christ was restricted to being in one place at any point in time, being confined to his human body; instead of knowing everything, Christ was restricted to knowing only as much as his human mind could contain; and instead of having the power to do anything in his will and in accordance to his nature, Christ was restricted to the physical capacities of his human frame. In this way, Christ could be said to be fully human as far as his active capacity and existence is concerned.[6] The following will show why this qualifier is an important one.

In what sense, then, is Christ also fully divine? We must aver that Christ is fully divine in that he has never lost the divine being, which was in his incarnation simply concealed beneath the human nature. Christ is divine in his dormant capacity and existence. Yet this remains a part of his total existence, so that Christ cannot be said to be merely human without also being divine. This we elect to call an *aspectual* theory of the two na-

---

[5] Luke 2:52.

[6] Perhaps Christ's omnipotence was handed over to the custodianship of the Holy Spirit, to be given approval and release for exercise by the Father, so that one is able to understand that Christ was not merely trying to be human by eschewing use of his divine powers but truly limited in the way human beings are.

tures of Christ in that the natures correspond to the aspects of his existence; the active in the case of the human and the dormant in the case of the divine.[7]

Support for this perspective may be found in John Zizioulas' early discussion of Christology, in which he highlights the fact that Christ's single personhood unites his divine and human natures, with the result that, just as Christ cannot be divided into two persons which contradict or oppose one another, so he cannot be divided into two natures which are mutually at variance in any way.[8] At the end of his paper, Zizioulas gives clearer expression to his significant insight.[9]

Under this scheme, it must be clarified and emphasized, while limits are set to the non-moral properties of the Son *qua* human being, the moral properties, qualities definitive of the divine character, remain unlimited and boundless in their perfection even in the active capacity and existence of Christ. This seems to be the necessary implication of the Lord's categorical claim before his disciples that the one who has seen him has also seen the Father.[10]

He could not have been referring merely to the teachings which he could deliver and miracles which he could perform by the agency of the Father and the Holy Spirit respectively, significant as these may be for the identification of the divine being. That which the Lord Jesus meant when he asserted his visible identity with the Father had to be his moral qualities, which were completely evinced even in his human form. Accordingly, we are held back from subscribing to a view of Christ as having wavered in his resolve at the garden of Gethsemane or having experienced some form of conflict between two inner selves.

Another reason that precludes a theory of Christ as possessing two natures, wills, and souls which are substantially different, such that the human nature is characterized by a certain degree of selfishness which is not found in the divine nature, is that this would be to posit an addition in substance to the divine being so that instead of there being simply one being, with the incarnation the divine being acquires a human substance as well that is attached to the second divine person of the Son. In contrast, the concept of the two natures of Christ as aspectual and of the human nature as a circumscription of the divine does not encounter such a difficulty.

---

[7] This seems to be the standpoint of Millard Erickson in *Christian Theology*, 3rd ed. (Grand Rapids, MI: Baker Academic, 2013), pp. 670–71.

[8] J. D. Zizioulas, 'Human Capacity and Human Incapacity: A Theological Exploration of Personhood', in *SJT* 28, no. 5 (October 1975), pp. 436–37.

[9] Ibid., p. 447.

[10] John 14:9.

A legitimate inquiry that could be made concerns whether the presence of perfect moral qualities compromises the humanness of Christ. No serious problem is arguably posed in this regard since the moral likeness and even identity of human beings with God is a scriptural presupposition[11] and expectation Christ has of his disciples.[12] There is no need in this respect overly to emphasize the distinction between Christ and other human beings whereby the former is by nature what the latter are by grace concerning being a son of God. To press the point is to risk falling afoul of the misconception that those who receive the Spirit of God and walk according to the leading of the Spirit lose their human nature by implication. What finally matters is that moral perfection is not antithetical to being human; in truth, it is the divine vision for humanity.

Yet, if the moral perfection of the Son is in no way concealed in the incarnate Christ, and completely revelatory of the moral perfection of the divine being as such, how is it that the essence of God continues to be inaccessible to human persons? This is so in light of the fact that though the moral qualities expressed and manifested in the active capacity and existence of Christ are qualitatively identical with those of the divine being, their boundlessness and infinity are not expressed in the active capacity and existence of Christ in any limited period of time, though moral perfection subsists to infinite degree even in his active human existence. As to why this is the case, it is for the reason that the boundless can only be expressed in the boundless. It is impossible for the infinite love of God, say, to be fully disclosed in the finite context of time and space.

Ethical Implications

A momentous result flows from the separateness of personal consciousness and being as well as the ability of the former to share in the latter, in some sense, of another. The personal experience of the Apostle Paul himself[13] indicates the Christian life as a tumultuous one where will is set against the wielding and domination of an entire being by a foreign power with its own will and rationality. Might it not be that when Paul vehemently disavows that foreign mind and will as his own,[14] he is thinking in terms of an alien being that has come into his existence, giving it 'content' for which it was not cre-

---

[11] God created human beings in his own image, with moral and rational capacity.
[12] Matt. 5:48, ESV.
[13] According to an interpretation of Rom. 7:13–25.
[14] Rom. 7:17, 20.

ated and producing mayhem? Could not the human being, in ethical terminology, be 'form' awaiting the 'substance' that comes from God by the Holy Spirit?

For this reason St. Peter is able to make marvelous claims,[15] to the effect that God has endowed human beings with the capacity to live as the Lord Jesus lived on earth. Perhaps this is why the Lord himself spoke of how he is in them even as the Father is in him.[16] That which he meant is that the wisdom and will of the Trinity, of the divine persons, is granted to human persons as they walk in accordance with the indwelling Spirit by the latter's active operation, permanently at the return of Christ and for spurts and periods prior to the same, without replacing their personal consciousness or memories, so that to all intents and purposes the person remains the same, except without the capacity to sin, and with the infallible capacity for righteousness.

Missional Implications

The notion of a mutual ontological dependence of the persons of the Godhead which does not detract from their possession of full personhood but indeed enables the same glorifies the idea of the Lord Jesus as the bodily temple of the fullness of the divine being.[17]

This is for the reason that if the Son, on whose unique principle the Father and the Holy Spirit eternally depend, were truly circumscribed and localized in a finite physical form as the scriptural doctrine of the incarnation claims, not just the Son but in a very real sense the Father and the Holy Spirit have undergone, within time though not within eternity, crucial transformation in their being in the form of a circumscription and localization of the faculty of the will so that the incarnate Son becomes the nexus of all divinity. This may serve to explain why the Lord, and his servant Paul, spoke of how the Father had entrusted his kingdom entirely into his hands, a state of affairs that will eventually change when the Son hands the kingdom back into the hands of his Father.

Such an understanding has immense consequences for the mission of the church as the body of Christ, for now the church is no longer simply directly related to the Lord and indirectly related to the Father, but as the historical and global human community which submits without reserve to the Lord Jesus, in whom dwell the Father and the Ho-

---

[15] In 2 Pet. 1:3–11, if Peter be at all its author.
[16] John 17:22–23.
[17] Col. 2:9.

ly Spirit, submits categorically to all three persons of the Godhead, the blessed Trinity. Jesus stands not only as a mediator between God and humankind who provides access to the Father by coming between them but, more importantly, embodies the very presence of the Father and the power of the Holy Spirit. The theory of *perichoretic constitution* thus imbues with new and vivid meaning the words of Christ that the one who receives his disciples receives him and by receiving him receives the Father.[18]

As the church worships and serves the Lord Christ, she worships and serves the Father, the Son, and the Holy Spirit in the unity of the divine being, one God, from eternity to eternity. The Christian community, then, need not fear that devoting worship exclusively to the Son might somehow deprive the Father of the reverence due to him as though the two were discrete and separate beings, given that such worship has been approved and as a matter of fact made possible by the Father, who stands beneath the Son as a necessary ontological factor in his being. In this way, the church is reminded that her commission is to summon the elect of the nations to worship Christ alone, through which activity the Father, and the Holy Spirit also receive worship.

Practical Implications

In addition to the scriptural, doctrinal, ethical, and missional dimensions, our ontological scheme of the immanent Trinity has certain implications for the Christian. Being mutually ontological dependent, the divine persons are aware of the debt of gratitude they owe to each other. They realize that without the other two, each of them would not be able to exist and function in the way they do. In a similar way, human persons are dependent on God, one another, and the rest of the created order.[19] To this may be added the similar discovery of African tradition which Priscilla Pope-Levison and John Levison note.[20]

There is therefore no room for presumptuousness and conceit. Instead, it is seemly for the human individual to cultivate an attitude of contentment in their different circumstances and stations of life. Amid consumeristic and gain-driven cultures that promote personal acquisition of material and social goods, the Christian scriptures relay a counter-cultural message through our specific understanding of the immanent Trinity:

---

[18] Matt. 10:40.

[19] J. D. Zizioulas, *Lectures in Christian Dogmatics* (London: T&T Clark, 2008), p. 26.

[20] P. Pope-Levison and J. R. Levison, *Jesus in Global Contexts* (Louisville, KY: Westminster/John Knox, 1992), p. 94.

Christians should receive the things they already have with utmost gratitude, for they account for their present existence and functioning, and pave the way for the future that God has in store for them.

Conclusion

In spite of its conceptual nature, the foregoing exploration has had one fundamental and practical concern at its heart: to enable Christians to comprehend and articulate the doctrine of the Trinity in a logically consistent manner. For those who maintain the reality of triple divine personhood, such as the ancient and modern theologians considered in this study, the challenge is to gather up the three in light of the one that is in God.

The above proposal is one way in which God may be defined as a single personal being; not as 'God-ness' or 'God-ity', but, indeed, as God. Given that aspects of the reality of God are in view, the proposal is necessarily speculative, showing, as those who believe in the logical coherence of the Christian faith owe it to themselves to do, within the limits of human ability, how it is possible to simultaneously maintain that there is but one God, yet three entities equally divine.[1]

Furthermore, the discussion has assumed from the outset the biblical basis of the classical doctrine of the Trinity. Suffice it to say that an ontological view of the divinity of Christ is clearly grounded in scripture, which proclaims his co-eternity with God and his instrumental role in creation and providence – acts ascribed only to God – attributes to him a nature that belongs to God, and identifies him with the divine being.[2]

It is hoped that the preceding examination, analysis, and synthesis would serve to everywhere endue proponents of classical Trinitarian doctrine with a greater measure of confidence in the rationality of their belief in the nature of God, who is the Father, the only God; the Son, the only God; and the Holy Spirit, the only God.

---

[1] J. S. Feinberg, *No One Like Him: The Doctrine of God*, Foundations of Evangelical Theology (Wheaton, IL: Crossway Books, 2001), p. 493.

[2] John 1:1–4; Heb. 1:1–3.

Bibliography

Alston, W. P. 'Substance and the Trinity'. In *The Trinity: An Interdisciplinary Symposium on the Trinity*, edited by S. T. Davis, D. Kendall, and G. O'Collins, 179–201. Oxford: Oxford University Press, 2002.

Anatolios, K. 'Personhood, Communion, and the Trinity in Some Patristic Texts'. In *The Holy Trinity in the Life of the Church*, Holy Cross Studies in Patristic Theology and History, edited by K. Anatolios, 147–64. Grand Rapids, MI: Baker Academic, 2014.

———. *Retrieving Nicaea: The Development and Meaning of Trinitarian Doctrine*. Grand Rapids, MI: Baker Academic, 2011.

Anselm of Canterbury. *St. Anselm: Basic Writings*. 2nd ed. Translated by S. N. Deane. Open Court Classics. La Salle, IL: Open Court, 1962.

Athanasius of Alexandria. 'Four Discourses Against the Arians'. In *Nicene and Post-Nicene Fathers*, Second Series 4, translated by J. H. Newman and A. Robertson, 303–447. New York: Cosimo Classics, 2007.

Audi, R., ed. *The Cambridge Dictionary of Philosophy*. 2nd ed. Cambridge: Cambridge University Press, 1999.

Augustine of Hippo. *The Trinity*. Translated by E. Hill. The Works of Saint Augustine: A Translation for the 21st Century. Hyde Park, NY: New City Press, 1990.

Ayres, L. 'On Not Three People: The Fundamental Themes of Gregory of Nyssa's Trinitarian Theology As Seen In *To Ablabius: On Not Three Gods*'. In *Re-thinking Gregory of Nyssa*, edited by S. Coakley, 15–44. Malden, MA: Blackwell, 2003.

———. *Augustine and the Trinity*. Cambridge: Cambridge University Press, 2010.

———. *Nicaea and Its Legacy: An Approach to Fourth-Century Trinitarian Theology*. Oxford: Oxford University Press, 2004.

Barnes, M. R. 'Augustine in Contemporary Trinitarian Theology'. *Theological Studies* 56 (1995): 237–50

———. 'Latin Trinitarian Theology'. In *The Cambridge Companion to The Trinity*, edited by P. C. Phan, 70–84. Cambridge: Cambridge University Press, 2011.

Basil of Caesarea. 'Letter XXXVIII'. In *Basil: The Letters 1—58*, translated by R. J. Deferrari, Loeb Classical Library 190, 196–227. Cambridge, MA: Harvard University Press, 1926.

———. 'Letter CCXIV'. In *Basil: The Letters 186—248*, translated by R. J. Deferrari, Loeb Classical Library 243, 226–37. Cambridge, MA: Harvard University Press, 1930.

———. 'Letter CCXXXVI'. In *Basil: The Letters 186—248*, translated by R. J. Deferrari, Loeb Classical Library 243, 386–405. Cambridge, MA: Harvard University Press, 1930.

———. 'Liber de Spiritu Sancto'. In *Patrologia Graeca*, edited by J.-P. Migne, vol. 32, 67–218. Paris, 1857–1886.

———. *On the Holy Spirit*. Translated by S. M. Hildebrand. Popular Patristics Series 42. Yonkers, NY: St. Vladimir's Seminary Press, 2011.

Bauer, W., F. W. Danker, W. F. Arndt, and F. W. Gingrich. *A Greek-English Lexicon of the New Testament and Other Early Christian Literature*. 3rd ed. Chicago: University of Chicago Press, 2000.

Beeley, C. A. 'Divine Causality and the Monarchy of God the Father in Gregory of Nazianzus'. *Harvard Theological Review* 100 (2007): 199–214. *ATLA Religion Database with ATLASerials*, EBSCO*host* (accessed February 28, 2015).

———. *Gregory of Nazianzus on the Trinity and the Knowledge of God: In Your Light We Shall See Light*. Oxford Studies in Historical Theology. Oxford: Oxford University Press, 2007.

Behr, J. *The Nicene Faith*. Vol. 2 of *The Formation of Christian Theology*. Crestwood, NY: St. Vladimir's Seminary Press, 2004.

Boethius. *Theological Tractates, The Consolation of Philosophy*. 2nd ed. Translated by H. F. Stewart, E. K. Rand, and S. J. Tester. Loeb Classical Library 74. Cambridge, MA: Harvard University Press, 1973.

Bovon, F. *Luke 3: A Commentary on the Gospel of Luke 19:28—24:53*. Translated by J. Crouch. Hermeneia. Minneapolis, MN: Fortress, 2012.

Bowra, C. M. *Classical Greece*. Great Ages of Man: A History of the World's Cultures. Amsterdam: Time-Life International (Nederland), 1965.

Bray, G. L. *The Doctrine of God*. Contours of Christian Theology. Downers Grove, IL: InterVarsity Press, 1993.

Bray, G. L., ed. *We Believe in One God*. Ancient Christian Doctrine 1. Downers Grove, IL: IVP Academic, 2009.

Brown, D. *The Divine Trinity*. La Salle, IL: Open Court, 1985.

Chester, T. *Delighting in the Trinity: Why Father, Son and Spirit are Good News*. 2nd ed. Surrey, UK: The Good Book, 2010.

Chiavone, M. L. *The One God: A Critically Developed Evangelical Doctrine of Trinitarian Unity*. Eugene, OR: Pickwick, 2009.

Coakley, S. ''Persons' in the 'Social' Doctrine of the Trinity: A Critique of Current Analytic Discussion'. In *The Trinity: An Interdisciplinary Symposium on the Trinity*, edited by S. T. Davis, D. Kendall, and G. O'Collins, 123–44. Oxford: Oxford University Press, 2002.

———. 'Why Three? Some Further Reflections on the Origins of the Doctrine of the Trinity'. In *The Making and Remaking of Christian Doctrine: Essays in Honour of Maurice Wiles*, edited by S. Coakley and D. A. Pailin. Oxford: Clarendon Press, 1993.

Coffey, D. *Deus Trinitas: The Doctrine of the Triune God*. New York: Oxford University Press, 1999.

Collins, P. M. *Trinitarian Theology: West and East: Karl Barth, the Cappadocian Fathers, and John Zizioulas*. Oxford: Oxford University Press, 2001.

Corrigan, K. 'Οὐσία and ὑπόστασις in the Trinitarian Theology of the Cappadocian Fathers: Basil and Gregory of Nyssa'. *Zeitschrift für Antikes Christentum* 12 (2008): 114–34. *ATLA Religion Database with ATLASerials*, EBSCO*host* (accessed February 28, 2015).

Craig, W. L. 'Toward a Tenable Social Trinitarianism'. In *Philosophical and Theological Essays on the Trinity*, edited by T. McCall and M. C. Rea, 89–99. Oxford: Oxford University Press, 2009.

Cross, R. 'Gregory of Nyssa on Universals'. In *Vigiliae Christianae* 56, no. 4 (2002): 372–410. *ATLA Religion Database with ATLASerials*, EBSCO*host* (accessed August 17, 2015).

Cunningham, D. S. *These Three Are One: The Practice of Trinitarian Theology*. Challenges in Contemporary Theology. Malden, MA: Blackwell, 1998.

Daley, B. E. 'Maximus the Confessor and John of Damascus on the Trinity'. In *The Holy Trinity in the Life of the Church*, edited by K. Anatolios, Holy Cross Studies in Patristic Theology and History, 79–99. Grand Rapids, MI: Baker Academic, 2014.

Deferrari, R. J. Introduction to *Basil: The Letters 1—58*, by Basil of Caesarea. Loeb Classical Library 190. Cambridge, MA: Harvard University Press, 1926.

———. *Basil: The Letters 186—248*. Loeb Classical Library 243. Cambridge, MA: Harvard University Press, 1930.

DeYoung, K. *The Good News We Almost Forgot: Rediscovering the Gospel in a 16th Catechism*. Chicago: Moody, 2010.

Dünzl, F. *A Brief History of the Doctrine of the Trinity in the Early Church*. Translated by J. Bowden. London: T&T Clark, 2007.

Edgar, B. *The Message of the Trinity: Life in God*. The Bible Speaks Today. Leicester, UK: Inter-Varsity, 2004.

Emery, G. and M. Levering. 'Prospects for Trinitarian Theology'. In *The Oxford Handbook of the Trinity*, edited by G. Emery and M. Levering, 600–605. Oxford: Oxford University Press, 2011.

Erickson, M. J. *Christian Theology*. 3rd ed. Grand Rapids, MI: Baker Academic, 2013.

———. *God in Three Persons: A Contemporary Interpretation of the Trinity*. Grand Rapids, MI: Baker Books, 1995.

Eunomius of Cyzicus. 'Liber Apologeticus'. In *Eunomius: The Extant Works*, translated by R. P. Vaggione, Oxford Early Christian Texts, 1–75. Oxford: Oxford University Press, 1987.

Fairbairn, D. *Life in the Trinity: An Introduction to Theology with the Help of the Church Fathers*. Downers Grove, IL: IVP Academic, 2009.

Fedwick, P. J. Foreword to *Gregory of Nyssa and the Concept of Divine Persons* by L. Turcescu, ix–xi. American Academy of Religion Academy Series. Oxford: Oxford University Press, 2005.

Feinberg, J. S. *No One Like Him: The Doctrine of God*. Foundations of Evangelical Theology. Wheaton, IL: Crossway Books, 2001.

Fiddes, P. S. 'Relational Trinity: Radical Perspective'. In *Two Views on the Doctrine of the Trinity*, edited by J. S. Sexton and S. N. Gundry, 159–85. Counterpoints. Grand Rapids, MI: Zondervan, 2014.

Fortman, E. J. *The Triune God: A Historical Study of the Doctrine of the Trinity*. Grand Rapids, MI: Baker Book House, 1972.

Fox, M. V. *Proverbs 1—9*. The Anchor Bible 18A. New Haven, CT: Yale University Press, 2000.

George, T. Introduction to *God the Holy Trinity: Reflections on Christian Faith and Practice*, edited by T. George. Grand Rapids, MI: Baker Academic, 2006.

Giles, K. *Jesus and the Father: Modern Evangelicals Reinvent the Doctrine of the Trinity*. Grand Rapids, MI: Zondervan, 2006.

Gioia, L. *The Theological Epistemology of Augustine's De Trinitate*. Oxford Theological Monographs. Oxford: Oxford University Press, 2008.

Gregory of Nazianzus. 'Oratio 29'. In *Patrologia Graeca*, edited by J.-P. Migne, vol. 36, 73–104. Paris, 1857–1886.

———. 'Oratio 31'. In *Patrologia Graeca*, edited by J.-P. Migne, vol. 36, 133–72. Paris, 1857–1886.

———. 'Oratio 42'. In *Patrologia Graeca*, edited by J.-P. Migne, vol. 36, 453–92. Paris, 1857–1886.

———. 'Oration 29: On the Son'. Translated by L. Wickham. In *On God and Christ: The Five Theological Orations and Two Letters to Cledonius*, Popular Patristics Series 23, 69–92. Crestwood, NY: St. Vladimir's Seminary Press, 2002.

———. 'Oration 31: On the Holy Spirit'. Translated by L. Wickham. In *On God and Christ: The Five Theological Orations and Two Letters to Cledonius*, Popular Patristics Series 23, 117–47. Crestwood, NY: St. Vladimir's Seminary Press, 2002.

———. 'Oration 39: On the Baptism of Christ'. In *Festal Orations*, translated by V. E. F. Harrison. Popular Patristics Series 36, 79–97. Crestwood, NY: St. Vladimir's Seminary Press, 2008.

———. 'Oration 40: On Baptism'. In *Festal Orations*, translated by V. E. F. Harrison. Popular Patristics Series 36, 99–142. Crestwood, NY: St. Vladimir's Seminary Press, 2008.

———. 'Oration XLII'. In *Nicene and Post-Nicene Fathers*, Second Series 7, translated by C. G. Browne and J. E. Swallow, 385–95. New York: Cosimo Classics, 2007.

Gregory of Nyssa. 'Ad Ablabium'. In *Patrologia Graeca*, edited by J.-P. Migne, vol. 45, 115–36. Paris, 1857–1886.

———. 'Ad Eustathium'. In *Gregorii Nysseni opera*, vol. 3.1, edited by F. Mueller, 3–16. Leiden, Netherlands: Brill, 1958.

———. 'Ad Graecos'. In Stramara, Jr., D. F. 'Gregory of Nyssa, *Ad Graecos "How It Is That We Say There Are Three Persons In The Divinity But Do Not Say There Are Three Gods"* (To The Greeks: Concerning The Commonality Of Concepts)', translated by Stramara, Jr., D. F., *Greek Orthodox Theological Review* 41, no. 4 (1996): 375–91, *ATLA Religion Database with ATLASerials*, EBSCO*host* (accessed September 2, 2015).

———. 'The Great Catechism'. In *Nicene and Post-Nicene Fathers*, Second Series 5, translated by W. Moore, 471–509. New York: Cosimo Classics, 2007.

———. 'To Ablabius'. In *Nicene and Post-Nicene Fathers*, Second Series 5, translated by H. A. Wilson, 331–36. New York: Cosimo Classics, 2007.

———. 'To Eustathius'. In *Nicene and Post-Nicene Fathers*, Second Series 5, translated by H. A. Wilson, 326–30. New York: Cosimo Classics, 2007.

Gregory Thaumaturgus. 'Expositio Fidei'. In *Patrologia Graeca*, edited by J.-P. Migne, vol. 10, 983–88. Paris, 1857–1886.

Gruenler, R. G. *The Trinity in the Gospel of John: A Thematic Commentary on the Fourth Gospel.* Eugene, OR: Wipf and Stock, 2004.

Gunton, C. E. *Act and Being: Towards a Theology of the Divine Attributes.* Grand Rapids, MI: William B. Eerdmans, 2003.

———. *Becoming and Being: The Doctrine of God in Charles Hartshorne and Karl Barth.* 2nd ed. London: SCM, 2001.

———. *Father, Son and Holy Spirit: Essays Toward a Fully Trinitarian Theology.* London: T&T Clark, 2003.

———. *The Christian Faith: An Introduction to Christian Doctrine.* Malden, MA: Blackwell, 2002.

———. *The Promise of Trinitarian Theology.* 2nd ed. London: T&T Clark, 1997.

Hanson, R. P. C. *The Search for the Christian Doctrine of God: The Arian Controversy, 318–381.* Grand Rapids, MI: Baker Academic, 2005.

Harrison, V. E. F. 'Illumined From All Sides By The Trinity: Neglected Themes in Gregory's Trinitarian Theology'. In *Re-Reading Gregory of Nazianzus: Essays on History, Theology, and Culture*, edited by C. A. Beeley, 13–30. CUA Studies in Early Christianity. Washington, D.C.: The Catholic University of America Press, 2012.

Heidegger, M. 'The Onto-Theo-Logical Constitution of Metaphysics'. In *Identity and Difference*, translated by J. Stambaugh, 42–76. Chicago: The University of Chicago Press, 2002.

Heltzel, P. G., and C. T. Collins Winn. 'Karl Barth, Reconciliation, and the Triune God'. In *The Cambridge Companion to The Trinity*, edited by P. C. Phan, 173–91. Cambridge: Cambridge University Press, 2011.

Hildebrand, S. M. *On the Holy Spirit*. Popular Patristics Series 42. Yonkers, NY: St. Vladimir's Seminary Press, 2011.

———. *The Trinitarian Theology of Basil of Caesarea: A Synthesis of Greek Thought and Biblical Truth*. Washington, DC: The Catholic University of America Press, 2006.

Holmes, S. R. 'Classical Trinity: Evangelical Perspective'. In *Two Views on the Doctrine of the Trinity*, edited by J. S. Sexton and S. N. Gundry, 25–48. Counterpoints. Grand Rapids, MI: Zondervan, 2014.

———. 'Trinitarian Action and Inseparable Operations: Some Historical and Dogmatic Reflections'. In *Advancing Trinitarian Theology: Explorations in Constructive Dogmatics*, edited by O. D. Crisp and F. Sanders, 60–74. Los Angeles Theology Conference. Grand Rapids, MI: Zondervan, 2014.

———. *The Quest for the Trinity: The Doctrine of God in Scripture, History and Modernity*. Downers Grove, IL: IVP Academic, 2012.

Jenson, R. W. *The Triune Identity: God According to the Gospel*. Philadelphia, PA: Fortress Press, 1982.

John of Damascus. *Saint John of Damascus: Writings*. Translated by F. H. Chase, Jr. The Fathers of the Church: A New Translation 37. Washington, DC: The Catholic University of America Press, 1958.

Jüngel, E. *God's Being Is In Becoming: The Trinitarian Being of God in the Theology of Karl Barth. A Paraphrase*. Translated by J. Webster. Grand Rapids, MI: William B. Eerdmans, 2001.

Kariatlis, P. 'St Basil's Contribution to the Trinitarian Doctrine: A Synthesis of Greek *Paideia* and the Scriptural Worldview'. *Phronema* 25 (2010): 57–83. *ATLA Religion Database with ATLASerials*, EBSCO*host* (accessed February 27, 2015).

Kärkkäinen, V.-M. *The Trinity: Global Perspectives*. Louisville, KY: Westminster John Knox, 2007.

Keller, T. *King's Cross: The Story of the World in the Life of Jesus*. London: Hodder, 2013.

———. *The Reason for God: Belief in an Age of Scepticism*. London: Hodder, 2009.

Kelly, D. F. *The God Who Is: The Holy Trinity*. Vol. 1 of *Systematic Theology: Grounded in Holy Scripture and Understood in the Light of the Church*. Ross-shire, Scotland: Mentor, 2008.

Lampe, G. W. H., ed. *A Patristic Greek Lexicon*. Oxford: Clarendon, 1961.

Law, J. T. *A Catechetical Exposition of the Apostles' Creed*. London: C. and J. Rivington, 1825.

Letham, R. 'Eternal Generation in the Church Fathers'. In *One God in Three Persons: Unity of Essence, Distinction of Persons, Implications for Life*, edited by B. A. Ware and J. Starke, 109–25. Wheaton, IL: Crossway, 2015.

———. *The Holy Trinity: In Scripture, History, Theology, and Worship*. Phillipsburg, NJ: P&R, 2004.

Liddell, H. G., R. Scott, and H. S. Jones, eds. *A Greek-English Lexicon*. 9th ed. 2 vols. Oxford: Oxford University Press, 1940.

Lienhard, J. T. '*Ousia* and *Hypostasis*: The Cappadocian Settlement and the Theology of 'One *Hypostasis*''. In *The Trinity: An Interdisciplinary Symposium on the Trinity*, ed. S. T. Davis, D. Kendall, and G. O'Collins, 99–121. Oxford: Oxford University Press, 2002.

Lossky, V. *The Mystical Theology of the Eastern Church*. Crestwood, NY: St. Vladimir's Seminary Press, 1976.

McCall, T. H. 'Relational Trinity: Radical Perspective: Response to Paul S. Fiddes'. In *Two Views on the Doctrine of the Trinity*, edited by J. S. Sexton and S. N. Gundry, 197–203. Counterpoints. Grand Rapids, MI: Zondervan, 2014.

———. 'Trinity Doctrine, Plain and Simple'. In *Advancing Trinitarian Theology: Explorations in Constructive Dogmatics*, edited by O. D. Crisp and F. Sanders, 42–59. Los Angeles Theology Conference. Grand Rapids, MI: Zondervan, 2014.

———. *Which Trinity? Whose Monotheism? Philosophical and Systematic Theologians on the Metaphysics of Trinitarian Theology*. Grand Rapids, MI: William B. Eerdmans, 2010.

Maspero, G. 'Trinity'. In *The Brill Dictionary of Gregory of Nyssa*, edited by L. F. Mateo-Seco and G. Maspero, translated by S. Cherney, 749–60. Supplements to Vigiliae Christianae: Texts and Studies of Early Christian Life and Language 99. Boston: Brill, 2010.

McGuckin, J. A. '"Perceiving Light from Light in Light' (*Oration* 31.3): The Trinitarian Theology of Saint Gregory the Theologian'. *Greek Orthodox Theological Review* 39, no. 1 (1994): 7–32. *ATLA Religion Database with ATLASerials*, EBSCO*host* (accessed August 13, 2015).

Meesters, A. C. 'The Cappadocians and Their Trinitarian Conceptions of God'. *Neue Zeitschrift Für Systematische Theologie Und Religionsphilosophie* 54, no. 4 (2012): 396–413. *ATLA Religion Database with ATLASerials*, EBSCO*host* (accessed August 1, 2015).

Meijering, E. P. *God Being History: Studies in Patristic Philosophy*. Amsterdam: North-Holland, 1975.

Meyendorff, J. *Byzantine Theology: Historical Trends and Doctrinal Themes*. 2nd ed. New York: Fordham University Press, 1983.

Moltmann, J. *The Trinity and the Kingdom: The Doctrine of God*. Translated by M. Kohl. Minneapolis, MN: Fortress Press, 1993.

Muller, R. A. *The Triunity of God*. Vol. 4 of *Post-Reformation Reformed Dogmatics: The Rise and Development of Reformed Orthodoxy, ca. 1520 to ca. 1725*. Grand Rapids, MI: Baker Academic, 2002.

Mullins, R. T. 'An Analytic Response to Stephen R. Holmes, with a Special Treatment of his Doctrine of Divine Simplicity'. In *The Holy Trinity Revisited: Essays in Response to Stephen R. Holmes*, edited by T. A. Noble and J. S. Sexton, 82–96. Christian Doctrines in Historical Perspective. Milton Keynes, England: Paternoster, 2015.

Norris, F. W. *Faith Gives Fullness to Reasoning: The Five Theological Orations of Gregory Nazianzen*. Supplements to Vigiliae Christianae 13. Leiden, Netherlands: E. J. Brill, 1991.

Olson, R. E. and C. A. Hall. *The Trinity*. Guides to Theology. Grand Rapids, MI: William B. Eerdmans, 2002.

Packer, J. I. *Knowing God*. London: Hodder & Stoughton, 2004.

Pannenberg, W. 'Eternity, Time, and the Trinitarian God'. In *Trinity, Time, and Church: A Response to the Theology of Robert W. Jenson*, edited C. E. Gunton, 62–70. Grand Rapids, MI: William B. Eerdmans, 2000.

Papanikolaou, A. 'Sophia, Apophasis, and Communion: the Trinity in Contemporary Orthodox Theology'. In *The Cambridge Companion to The Trinity*, edited by P. C. Phan, 243–58. Cambridge: Cambridge University Press, 2011.

Phan, P. C. 'Developments of the Doctrine of the Trinity'. In *The Cambridge Companion to The Trinity*, edited by P. C. Phan, 3–12. Cambridge: Cambridge University Press, 2011.

Pope-Levison, P., and J. R. Levison. *Jesus in Global Contexts*. Louisville, KY: Westminster/John Knox, 1992.

Prestige, G. L. *God in Patristic Thought*. Eugene, OR: Wipf & Stock, 2008.

Radde-Gallwitz, A. *Basil of Caesarea, Gregory of Nyssa, and the Transformation of Divine Simplicity*. Oxford Early Christian Studies. Oxford: Oxford University Press, 2009.

Rahner, K. *The Trinity*. Translated by J. Donceel. New York: Crossroad, 1997.

Richard of St. Victor. *On the Trinity*. Translated by R. Angelici. Eugene, OR: Cascade Books, 2011.

Sanlon, P. *Simply God: Recovering the Classical Trinity*. Nottingham, England: Inter-Varsity, 2014.

Seitz, C. R. *Word Without End: The Old Testament as Abiding Theological Witness*. Grand Rapids, MI: William B. Eerdmans, 1998.

Sexton, J. S. 'Conclusion'. In *Two Views on the Doctrine of the Trinity*, edited by J. S. Sexton and S. N. Gundry, 207–216. Counterpoints. Grand Rapids, MI: Zondervan, 2014.

Smail, T. A. *Like Father, Like Son: The Trinity Imaged in Our Humanity*. Milton Keynes, UK: Paternoster, 2005.

———. *Reflected Glory: The Spirit in Christ and Christians*. London: Hodder and Stoughton, 1977.

Stramara, Jr., D. F. 'Gregory of Nyssa, *Ad Graecos "How It Is That We Say There Are Three Persons In The Divinity But Do Not Say There Are Three Gods"* (To The Greeks: Concerning The Commonality Of Concepts)'. *Greek Orthodox Theological Review* 41, no. 4 (1996): 375–91. *ATLA Religion Database with ATLASerials*, EBSCO*host* (accessed September 2, 2015).

Sumner, D. O. 'Obedience and Subordination in Karl Barth's Trinitarian Theology'. In *Advancing Trinitarian Theology: Explorations in Constructive Dogmatics*, edited by O. D. Crisp and F. Sanders, 130–46. Los Angeles Theology Conference. Grand Rapids, MI: Zondervan, 2014.

Tanner, K. *Jesus, Humanity and the Trinity: A Brief Systematic Theology*. Scottish Journal of Theology: Current Issues in Theology. Edinburgh: T&T Clark, 2001.

Te Velde, R. A. 'The Divine Person(s): Trinity, Person, and Analogous Naming'. In *The Oxford Handbook of the Trinity*, edited by G. Emery and M. Levering, 359–70. Oxford: Oxford University Press, 2011.

Thomas Aquinas. *Summa theologica*. Translated by Fathers of the English Dominican Province. London: Burns Oates & Washbourne, 1920.

Torrance, T. F. *The Christian Doctrine of God: One Being, Three Persons*. London: T&T Clark, 1996.

———. *The Trinitarian Faith: The Evangelical Theology of the Ancient Catholic Church*. London: T&T Clark, 1991.

Turcescu, L. '"Person" versus "Individual", and Other Modern Misreadings of Gregory of Nyssa'. In *Re-thinking Gregory of Nyssa*, edited by S. Coakley, 97–109. Malden, MA: Blackwell, 2003.

———. 'Person'. In *The Brill Dictionary of Gregory of Nyssa*, edited by L. F. Mateo-Seco and G. Maspero, translated by S. Cherney, 591–96. Supplements to Vigiliae Christianae: Texts and Studies of Early Christian Life and Language 99. Boston: Brill, 2010.

———. *Gregory of Nyssa and the Concept of Divine Persons*. American Academy of Religion Academy Series. Oxford: Oxford University Press, 2005.

Vaggione, R. P. *Eunomius: The Extant Works*. Oxford Early Christian Texts. Oxford: Oxford University Press, 1987.

Volf, M. *After Our Likeness: The Church as the Image of the Trinity*. Sacra Doctrina. Grand Rapids, MI: Eerdmans, 1998.

Ware, B. A. 'A Modified Calvinist Doctrine of God'. In *Perspectives on the Doctrine of God: 4 Views*, edited by B. A. Ware, 76–120. Nashville, TN: B&H Academic, 2008.

———. *Father, Son, and Holy Spirit: Relationships, Roles and Relevance*. Wheaton, IL: Crossway Books, 2005.

Wilson, H. A. 'His Teaching on the Holy Trinity'. In *Gregory of Nyssa: Dogmatic Treatises*. Nicene and Post-Nicene Fathers Second Series 5, 23–9. New York: Cosimo Classics, 2007.

Yandell, K. 'How Many Times Does Three Go Into One?' In *Philosophical and Theological Essays on the Trinity*, edited by T. McCall and M. C. Rea, 151–68. Oxford: Oxford University Press, 2009.

Zachhuber, J. 'Once Again: Gregory of Nyssa on Universals'. *Journal of Theological Studies* ns 56 no 1 (April 2005): 75–98. *ATLA Religion Database with ATLASerials*, EBSCO*host* (accessed August 16, 2015).

———. *Human Nature in Gregory of Nyssa: Philosophical Background and Theological Significance*. Boston: Brill, 2014.

Zizioulas, J. D. 'Human Capacity and Human Incapacity: A Theological Exploration of Personhood'. *Scottish Journal of Theology* 28, no. 5 (October 1975): 401–447.

———. 'On Being a Person: Towards an Ontology of Personhood'. In *Persons, Divine and Human: King's College Essays in Theological Anthropology*, edited by C. Schwöbel and C. E. Gunton, 33–46. Edinburgh: T&T Clark, 1991.

———. 'The Doctrine of the Holy Trinity: The Significance of the Cappadocian Contribution'. In *Trinitarian Theology Today: Essays on Divine Being and Act*, edited by C. Schwöbel and C. E. Gunton, 44–60. Edinburgh: T&T Clark, 1995.

———. *Being as Communion: Studies in Personhood and the Church*. Contemporary Greek Theologians 4. Crestwood, NY: St. Vladimir's Seminary Press, 1985.

———. *Communion and Otherness: Further Studies in Personhood and the Church*. London: T&T Clark, 2006.

———. *Lectures in Christian Dogmatics*. London: T&T Clark, 2008.